HOMER

THE
ILIAD

NOTES

COLES EDITORIAL BOARD

Bound to stay open

Publisher's Note

Otabind (Ota-bind). This book has been bound using the patented Otabind process. You can open this book at any page, gently run your finger down the spine, and the pages will lie flat.

ABOUT COLES NOTES

COLES NOTES have been an indispensible aid to students on five continents since 1948.

COLES NOTES are available for a wide range of individual literary works. Clear, concise explanations and insights are provided along with interesting interpretations and evaluations.

Proper use of COLES NOTES will allow the student to pay greater attention to lectures and spend less time taking notes. This will result in a broader understanding of the work being studied and will free the student for increased participation in discussions.

COLES NOTES are an invaluable aid for review and exam preparation as well as an invitation to explore different interpretive paths.

COLES NOTES are written by experts in their fields. It should be noted that any literary judgement expressed herein is just that — the judgement of one school of thought. Interpretations that diverge from, or totally disagree with any criticism may be equally valid.

COLES NOTES are designed to supplement the text and are not intended as a substitute for reading the text itself. Use of the NOTES will serve not only to clarify the work being studied, but should enhance the reader's enjoyment of the topic.

ISBN 0-7740-3275-8

© COPYRIGHT 1993 AND PUBLISHED BY
COLES PUBLISHING COMPANY
TORONTO—CANADA
PRINTED IN CANADA

Manufactured by Webcom Limited
Cover finish: Webcom's Exclusive **Duracoat**

CONTENTS

CLASSICAL AND MYCENAEAN ARMOR

ABOVE: Traditional concept of Homeric heroes established centuries later in paintings and statuary of "Classical" Greece.

RIGHT: Armor used in the Trojan War; illustration based upon a suit of Mycenaean armor discovered recently at Dendra:

A. **HELMET**........bronze or leather, with matched carved boar's tusks sewn on, and horse-tail for decoration. **NOTE:** no visor or neck guard.

B. **SWORD**............worn over shoulder, size and design determined by owner.

C. **SHIELD**...."figure-eight" design, leather stretched over framework of sticks.

D. **CORSLET**.......bronze, with traditional Gorgon's head believed to avert evil.

E. **APRON**.......soft leather, design and style reflecting the taste of the owner.

F. **GREAVES**...........leather or bronze, attached by thongs, to guard the shins.

SOURCE: <u>Archeological</u> <u>Reports</u> 1960-61 pages 9-11; Frank H. Stubbings'
"Arms and Armor" in Wace and Stubbings' <u>A Companion</u> <u>to Homer</u> pages 504-522.

GREECE and the Aegean

THRACE

MACEDONIA

TROY

TROAD

Lemnos

Lesbos

MT. OLYMPOS

THESSALY

Skyros

Chios

HELLAS

EUBOEA

AULIS
BOEOTIA

THEBES

DELPHI

ATTICA

ATHENS

Cyclades

CORINTH

Delos

MYCENAE

ARGOS

ARCADIA

Melos

SPARTA

PYLOS

Scale: 100 miles

Ios

KNOSSOS

Crete   TYLISSOS

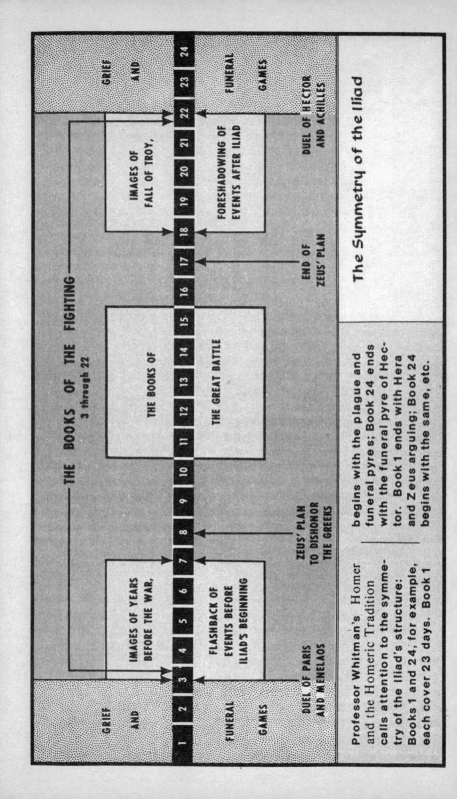

THE BOOKS OF THE FIGHTING
3 through 22

GRIEF AND

FUNERAL

GAMES

DUEL OF PARIS AND MENELAOS

IMAGES OF YEARS BEFORE THE WAR,

FLASHBACK OF EVENTS BEFORE ILIAD'S BEGINNING

ZEUS' PLAN TO DISHONOR THE GREEKS

THE BOOKS OF

THE GREAT BATTLE

END OF ZEUS' PLAN

IMAGES OF FALL OF TROY,

FORESHADOWING OF EVENTS AFTER ILIAD

GRIEF AND

FUNERAL

GAMES

DUEL OF HECTOR AND ACHILLES

The Symmetry of the Iliad

Professor Whitman's Homer and the Homeric Tradition calls attention to the symmetry of the Iliad's structure: Books 1 and 24, for example, Book 1 —— begins with the plague and funeral pyres; Book 24 ends with the funeral pyre of Hector. Book 1 ends with Hera and Zeus arguing; Book 24 begins with the same, etc.

PLOT DIAGRAM

	I	II	III	IV	V	VI	VII	VIII	IX	X	XI	XII	XIII	XIV	XV	XVI	XVII	XVIII	XIX	XX	XXI	XXII	XXIII	XXIV
LOCATION	Greek camp		outside Troy				plain of Troy						Greek camp			outside Troy	Greek camp		plain of Troy				Greek camp	Greek camp & Troy
AGAMEMNON	Offends Apollo and Achilles; Throws army into chaos						Order to fortify camp		Sends Embassy to Achilles		Wounded													
ACHILLES	Withdraws; asks vengeance through Thetis								Refuses plea to fight		Sends Patroklos for news					Turns back Trojans and is killed		Anger and grief / Reconciliation with Achilles	Goes into battle	Aristeia of Achilles		Kills Hektor	Funeral	
PATROKLOS											Comes to sympathize													
DIOMEDES					Aristeia of Diomedes					Night raid / Wounded														
MENELAOS			Duels with Paris	Shot by Pandaros			Into battle																	
PARIS			Duels with Menelaos																					
PRIAM			On the wall																			Pleads with Hektor		Claims body of Hektor
HEKTOR						Asks mother to pray to Athena / Into battle		Camps on plain			Aristeia of Hektor			Stunned by rock	Threatens Greeks with fire			Camps on plain				Death		funeral
TIME	23 days		4 days							1 night							4 days							23 days

BATTLE

GREEKS — TROJANS

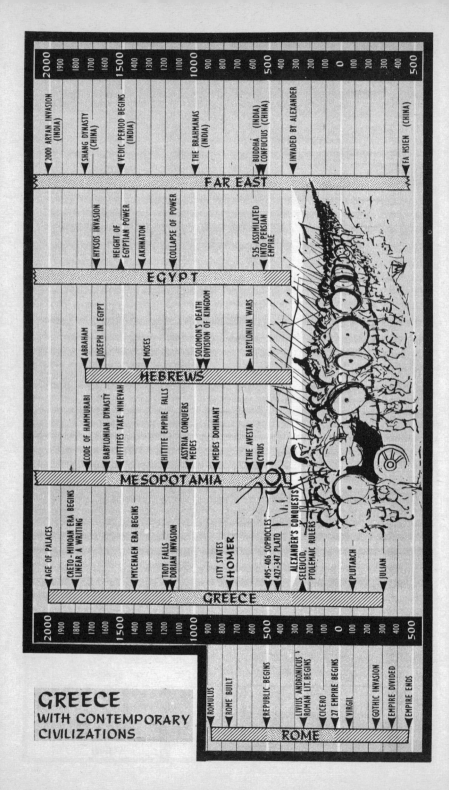

GREECE WITH CONTEMPORARY CIVILIZATIONS

HOMER: BIOGRAPHY OF LEGEND

It is unfortunate that we are sure of nothing about Homer. The ancient Greeks themselves seem to have known very little, but, as was often the case with honored men, many stories were circulated about him. These may be wholly fiction, but they may also contain some truth; we will probably never find out.

Several ancient cities claimed to be the birthplace of Homer, and there was similar disagreement about the time when he lived. It is generally agreed by scholars today that he was born somewhere in Ionia (the Greek west coast of Asia Minor), probably during the eighth century B.C. There may be some truth in the story of his blindness, for if the ancient tradition that Homer was the author of the Hymn to Delian Apollo is true, then he was blind. Near the end of the Hymn, the poet speaks to the girls who serve the Temple of Apollo on Delos:

> "Think of me in the future, whenever any person
> who has much experience comes here and asks you,
> 'Girls, which man sings most sweetly of the bards
> who come here, and whom do you like most to hear?'
> You must answer all together: 'A blind man, who lives
> in stony Chios, and whose songs will always be the
> finest.' "

There are references to his death in later Greek writers, but they may be based on traditions handed down from an earlier period. One account says that Homer "travelled from one city to another as a minstrel, and went to Delphi to ask what country was his fatherland." The oracle replied that he had no fatherland, but that he would be buried on the island of Ios (a very small island about halfway between Athens and Crete), and added that he should "watch out for the riddle of the young children". For many years after this he avoided Ios and continued his travels, during which he became very famous. When he was quite old, he went to Ios to join his son-in-law (nothing is known of his wife or daughter). The story continues:

> "And, they say, as he was sitting near the sea, he asked
> some boys who had been fishing, 'Gentlemen, hunters
> of sea-beasts, did we get anything?' They answered,

'As much as we caught, we left there, and as much as
we did not catch, we are carrying with us.' Since Homer
didn't understand this, he asked what they meant.
They replied that they hadn't caught any fish, but
had picked the lice off of themselves, and the ones
they caught they left there, but the ones they didn't
catch they were carrying in their clothes. Then Homer
remembered the oracle, and, realizing that the end
of his life had come, composed an epitaph for himself. He began to walk away, but it was muddy, and
he slipped and fell on his side. And, they say, he died
on the third day after this. He was buried on Ios. This
is the epitaph he composed: 'Here the earth hides the
holy head of the man who honored heroes, divine
Homer.' "

Although these stories about Homer are probably no
more than legends, and can furnish no real evidence for his
life, we do know something about the period in which he
probably lived (see "Homer's Ionia," below).

COMPLETE BACKGROUND

Introduction

An epic, Aristotle says, is a poem about men in action.
Ezra Pound, a modern poet and student of the classical tradition, defines the form as "a poem containing history." As will be
seen, the archaeological discovery of the ruins of Troy has con-
firmed the basic accuracy of Homer's account, but "action" is
the real concern of both the poet and today's reader. The *Iliad*
and the *Odyssey* reflect what was known of the geography of
the eastern Mediterranean; but, more important, they reflect
the character of every people known to the Greeks, and veritably
every human activity and emotion. In the *Iliad*, although the city
of Troy as setting would seem to limit Homer's scope, it is here
that the world's greatest heroes and gods convene. Few works
of literature have managed to achieve so broad a panorama of
scene, national character, and human emotion; in this, the *Iliad*
and the *Odyssey* rival Cervantes' *Don Quixote*, the plays of
Shakespeare, Tolstoy's *War and Peace*. Humanity will always
live with the questions, "What is a good man? A good woman?
A good society?" Homer's answers are of permanent value.

Indeed, the greatness of the poetry lies in its wise attitude toward the life of man. This, in turn, is enhanced by the matchless skill with which the story is told: never hurriedly, and yet never with a wasted word. Its diction is simple and exact; its lines, compact with action and detail. While three lines removed at random from a modern novel (or poem) may quite likely be obscure and even incomprehensible, three lines removed at random from Homer are invariably comprehensible, frequently even memorable.

The Historical Background

Mycenaean Greece   Achilles and Odysseus, Menelaos and Agamemnon, Helen and Paris, historical or not, are figures of the late Bronze Age in Greece in the twelfth century B.C. For Homer, in the eighth century, they represented a distant past which had become so glorified in song and legend as to be "heroic." History confirms that these Mycenaeans were indeed a mighty people: in the last generations before the "Dorian Invasion" (see below) they had extended a military and economic domain to include the islands of the Aegean, the Crete of the older Minoan empire, and even seem to have attacked Egypt. The Mycenaeans even knew and used the art of writing (see "The Linear B Tablets," below); they built mighty palaces of stone and had a political geography, the complexity of which is indicated in the *Iliad's* famous "Catalogue of Ships" and which is substantiated (though with altered particulars) in the written records found in the Mycenaean capitals of Pylos and Mycenae itself and in the Mycenaean-occupied Knossos on Crete (see MAP, p. 5).

Geography in Homer   In the eighteenth and early nineteenth centuries, it was thought that the world Homer describes was hardly more real than Alice's Wonderland. Though Athens is mentioned in both the epics, and Sparta (also called by its alternate name Lacedaimon) and several other locations still exist, it was assumed that Mycenae, Troy, and the fabulous cities of Crete (such as Knossos and Phaistos) were entirely mythical. In 1870, however, Heinrich Schliemann (1822-1890) began to dig in Turkey at a site which Homer's text seemed to indicate, and uncovered a burned city of some antiquity which he called Troy. Although he had not dug down far enough, and had actually discovered a much later city built over Troy's ruins, he is given credit for the discovery.

Six years later, Schliemann went to the Greek mainland and uncovered Agamemnon's city Mycenae, to the astonishment of the world. Here he found many golden weapons and containers, together with what has been traditionally called the golden death-mask of Agamemnon. In 1881, he uncovered Orchomenos and in 1885, Tiryns, cities in the Argive plain, both mentioned in the *Iliad*.

Between 1900 and 1908, Sir Arthur Evans (1851-1941), a British archaeologist, uncovered the beautiful Cretan palace of Minos at Knossos. Carl W. Blegen, the American archaeologist, has discovered and excavated sandy Pylos, Nestor's palace and city. These and other discoveries of this century have changed the entire conception of the reality of Homer's world, for suddenly it was not only very real but utterly strange and beautiful —and nothing at all like the Greece of Athens in the classical fifth century.

Linear B Script   The archaeologists however, gave us only the physical presence of Homer's world. It had no voice until Michael Ventris, a young English architect and amateur linguist, cracked the writing that had been found by Sir Arthur Evans at Knossos and Carl Blegen at Pylos—the famous Linear B script (so named to distinguish it from the earlier Linear A; the script itself is that used by the "Minoans," whose language continues to defy decipherment).

Ventris' discovery in 1952 shook the scholarly world, for it established (a) that Cretans in late Minoan times were familiar with a Greek vocabulary, for much of the Linear B is recognizable Greek written in a different and earlier alphabet (the Greek alphabet itself evolved much later out of contact with the Phoenicians), and (b) that Crete, far from being a separate empire from mainland Greece, was, just as Homer says, part of a large empire of Minoan and Mycenaean people, with the capitals of a system of kingdoms at Mycenae, Pylos, and Knossos. It used to be thought preposterous that Homer, "whoever he was," could write. We now know, however, that the written word was an important part of this distant past (the tablets at Pylos seem to have been written some four or five hundred years *before* Homer). The approximately 3500 tablets which have been recovered are inventories of cattle, ships, armour (all like Homer's own catalogues); the interested student should investigate the writings of John Chadwick, Leonard R. Palmer, and Joseph Alsop in the BIBLIOGRAPHY.

The People in Homer   The late Mycenaean world which Homer's poetry celebrates had existed centuries before him, and his knowledge of those times would have come from the oral tradition and other epics. Through modern archaeology, however, we may know more about the twelfth-century world of Homer's characters than he did himself in the eighth century.

"Kings," for example, in that "heroic" era, were no more than tribal chieftains. They maintained loose leagues among themselves for commercial intercourse and periodic common defense, but politics seem to have been otherwise quite primitive. Sculpture was somewhat crude and, for the most part, religious; vases and urns were decorated but these, too, were more functional than artistic. Weapons were bronze and wooden spears, bows and arrows (see illustration, p. 4). For a careful discussion of these early arts, see Friedrich Matz's *The Art of Crete and Early Greece.*

Neither were there great cities at this time; the mainland kings lived in fortified stone citadels and the townspeople in villages outside the walls, coming into the royal stronghold only in time of war. The remains of some of these citadels— Mycenae, Tiryns, and Pylos—furnish much information; many details are as Homer describes them.

There has been much speculation over the centuries about the appearance of Homer's heroes. The conventions of painting, of book illustrations, and of heroic statuary have provided the physical details of the traditional character, but archaeology has changed a great deal of this conception. For example, the famous horse-mane helmet, with its curved crest mounted above a helmet with visor and cheek-pieces, is much later than Achilles, time. Achilles, we now know, would have worn a peaked leather cap with small bronze or boar's tusk ivory plates sewn to it like fish scales and resembling medieval chain mail. The attached horse tail hung from the top and trailed down the warrior's back. His other armor would have been similarly mounted on leather. His clothes would have been brightly colored and embroidered with geometric designs; brief shirts were the undergarment; in cold weather woolen cloaks were worn and sandals were exchanged for warm boots.

Homer testifies that the Achaeans (his name for all Greeks) were a clean people, and honored the beauty of the body. They had no soap, but bathed in tubs of warm water and annointed themselves with a perfumed oil, the manufacture of which was the chief industry of the Mycenaean-Minoan Empire. We are not sure of what racial strain these people were. Many of them (Odysseus, Menelaos, and Helen, for instance) had hair that was yellow or red, certainly blond.

The best source nevertheless, for knowing *how* Homer's people lived is still Homer's poems, for it must be remembered that they are *poetic* people: the *Iliad is* literature. And yet we are offered great and reliable detail as to the practice of religion and sacrifices to and attitudes toward the gods, interiors of the dwellings, ships, clothing and foods—the physical realities of everyday life almost 3,000 years ago.

The Gods in Homer   The Greeks differed from the Greeks themselves in that the gods were immortal and were endowed with magical powers—there was little else to distinguish them from the lusty, jealous, hateful, hungry, and thirsty human beings below the not-so-lofty Mount Olympos. Literally, too, were the gods akin to men: many of the Greek gods were notorious in their seduction of the mortals. and in many an epic a mythical human being takes great pride in his superhuman lineage. The behavior of the gods, however. did not fully determine the character of religious observance which was, officially, most reverent.

The Greeks had no "churches" in the modern sense. The magnificent temples (so many of which still stand) were merely lodging for the particular god if he happened to be in the vicinity. The people never entered them except to offer sacrifices. In this sense, every man was a "priest" and all took part in the ritual. No part of the Greek day was excluded from religious observance of some sort, so much so that the Greeks had no sense of religion as an activity distinct from the rest of life: religion and everyday life were one.

There were twelve Olympian gods (whose home was a

city atop Mount Olympos), the king of whom was *Zeus* (whose name means simply "The Bright One"). Of these gods, Homer makes reference to *Pallas Athena,* goddess of the intelligence; *Aphrodite,* goddess of love; *Apollo,* god of light, music, and healing; *Ares,* god of war; *Poseidon,* god of the sea; *Artemis,* god of animals; *Hera,* goddess of mothers; *Hermes,* god of voyages; *Hebe,* goddess of children; and *Hephaistos,* god of fire.

Among the gods of the underworld were *Demeter,* goddess of ripened grain; her daughter *Persephone,* goddess of plant fertility; and *Dionysos,* god of wine. Because this Chthonic ("underground") religion was one of great mystery and secretiveness, we know far less about it than we do of the official public Zeus-religion.

Then there were countless minor dieties, such as *Leukothea,* a sea nymph who helps Odysseus, and *Thetis,* the sea-nymph mother of Achilles who entreats Zeus on his behalf. In fact, everything growing or moving was or contained an immortal spirit: springs, rivers, trees, the sun, moon, sea, and the mountains all were gods. The world was the Greek "church," and every phenomenon was interpreted as divinity in action.

The Dorian Invasions   Through the height of power and the twilight of the Mycenaean Age a people from the north of Greece, the Dorians, had been slowly and peacefully moving down into the Greek mainland. At this same time, the Mycenaean civilization was weakening from internal strife (as represented by the war against Thebes in the *Theban Cycle*—see "Other Greek Epics," below) and by wars waged for wealth against the Trojans and others. The ten-year Trojan war was hardly a victory for the Mycenaeans, who seem to have exhausted themselves; the end of the war was followed by an increase in pressure from the Dorians and about 1100 B.C. came an almost total conquest of the Greek mainland and the Peloponesseus. The great cities of Mycenae, Pylos, and Tiryns, for example, were totally destroyed; only Athens was able to withstand the Dorians and remain a center of Mycenaean culture.

The Dark Ages and   From about 1100 to 800 B.C. is the period
the Ionian Migration   of the so-called "Dark Age" of Greek history, "dark" because we know very little of the times: rough, crude pottery is the only real record

we have of this "sub-Mycenaean" culture. The art of writing was forgotten and the great stone palaces were replaced with mud brick structures.

All traces of the Mycenaeans, however, were not wiped out in the invasion and occupation. The "Ionian Migration," a slow movement of people from the Greek mainland to the west coast of Asia Minor, took with it, preserved, and continued to develop the older culture.

Homer's Ionia   The eighth-century world in which Homer lived, though little more than four centuries distant from that of his Mycenaean heroes, contrasted greatly with that of his Mycenaean heroes, contrasted greatly with that "heroic" age. The Ionian civilization was one of a highly-developed sophistication in sipte of its being predominantly agricultural. Having lost the older, Linear B writing, they adapted the Phoenician alphabet and inaugurated a cultural revival.

The Ionians founded cities which were completely independent of each other and of the mainland. Most of the citizens were farmers and herdsmen (in the *Odyssey* there is the careful distinction between shepherds, swineherds, and goatherds—so specialized was their agrarian society). There were merchants and sailors, since trade with other areas in the Mediterranean area was reviving, and there were many craftsmen: carpenters, potters, and armorers; there is no evidence for large shops, however, and most essentials were made in the homes.

One of the classes of specialists was that of the wandering bards (*aoidoi*), such as Homer, who made their living by travelling through the various Greek settlements, reciting their versions of the epics or "songs" which celebrated the Mycenaean past as do the *Iliad* and *Odyssey*.

As well as giving us an idea of life in Mycenaean times, these epics also furnish us with evidence about life in Homer's own time. It is especially in the similes and descriptive passages that the life and preoccupations of Ionian Greeks in the eighth century are revealed.

The Making of the Epic

The Composition   Some of the songs recited by the *aoidoi* seem to have been preserved since Mycenaean times; others undoubtedly originated during the Dark

Age. Homer thus worked in a literary tradition very like that of the modern ballad singer and was free to quote lines and even long passages that existed in other ballads or poems. Homer's materials, as writing had been lost, had been preserved orally; the tales were memorized and sung from memory so that, through the generations, many changes in the materials were undoubtably lost, changed, or fabricated. Quotations from Homer in the texts of Aristophanes, Plato, and Aristotle show that their "Homer" was widely variant from that which has come down to us. For a discussion of the method of oral composition, see "The Epic Formula," below.

Other Greek Epics   Scholars now generally believe that the following epics were all written after Homer's *Iliad* and *Odyssey*. Both Homer and the others, however, took their plots and characters from pre-existing materials of the oral tradition. The later poets have attempted to supply enough information to Homer to complete the *Trojan* or *Homeric Cycle*: a telling of the stories of the war and its aftermath in a chronological and complete account. Several epic cycles seem to have existed, dealing with the adventures of *Theseus* (who slew the Minotaur in the Labyrinth of King Minos' palace), of *Perseus* (who slew the snake-haired gorgon Medusa), and of *Minos* (who owned the monstrous human flesh-eating bull from the sea). There were lengthy legends dealing with *Bellerophon* (who rode the winged horse Pegasus and slew the Chimaera) and with the great labors of *Herakles;* the *Argonautica* which dealt with the adventures of *Jason* and his men of Argos who sailed into a land of fantasy (very like that of the *Odyssey*) in search of the fabulous golden fleece. We know, too, of the *Theban Cycle*, three epics dealing with *King Oedipos* of Thebes, the curse his crime of patricide and marriage of his mother brought upon that city and the later battle for the city by Oedipos' sons in the "Seven Against Thebes" epic. Many of these epics have been lost and their authors are either unknown or disputed; references to the epics by other or later authors are often the only inkling of their existence (the "Theban Cycle" is no longer extant but is reported to have been preserved by Sophocles in his Oedipos Trilogy, the fifth-century plays *Oedipos Rex, Antigone,* and *Oedipos at Colonos.*

As it can be reconstructed, the *Homeric Cycle* seems to have consisted of some eight epics: (1) the KYPRIA celebrated the flight of Paris and Helen from Sparta before the outbreak of the war; it contains the story of the judgment of Paris after the wedding of Thetis at which Athena, Hera, and Aphrodite quarreled over who was to claim the golden apple inscribed "for the fairest." (b) the ILIAD of Homer describes approximately fifty days of the war. (c) the AITHIOPIS was a continuation of the war, from the funeral of Hektor to the death of Achilles. (d) the ILIAS PARVA ("the little Iliad") offers the account of Odysseus' Trojan Horse ruse to enter the city, the contest for Achilles' armor between Aïas and Odysseus. (e) the ILIU PERSIS portrayed the sack of Troy, the entrance into the battle of Achilles' son, the deaths of Hecuba, Priam, the rape and abduction of Kassandra, etc. (f) the NOSTOI describes the homeward voyages of the various Greek leaders (with the exception of Odysseus) and the fates they meet at their homes—here the murder of Agamemnon by his unfaithful wife is described to be recounted in Aeschylos' fifth-century drama. (g) the ODYSSEY of Homer, the *nostos*, "homeward voyage," of Odysseus. (h) the TELEGONIA, named after its main figure, Telegonos, a son of Odysseus by Circe, who slays his father and eventually marries Penelope; this epic closes the *Homeric Cycle* with the marriage of Telemakhos (Odysseus' son by Penelope) and Circe— all four go to live on Circe's enchanted isle.

The Epic Formula   The oral phase through which the epics
                            came in the Dark Age established a certain
poetic technique required by the recitations of the bards or singers. The plots of the stories were traditional by Homer's time and known to all, but the epics were not repeated verbatim—the plot or framework was established and unalterable, but the details seem to have varied with each re-telling.

Approximately one-third of the lines in Homer's poetry are repeated one or more times. The repetition is made possible by the uniform metrical pattern of hexameter lines (eight accented feet to the line) which never conclude with a broken thought; grammatical clauses are rarely continued from one line to another so that the language operates in neat formulas. Lines and verses may appear in whole, then, many times, their insertion never disrupting the flow of the tight metrical rhythm. Within the single lines are similarly formulized phrases of a fixed metrical count, facilitating the repetition of the phrase. Thus, for each poetic situation, there are epithet-name compounds ready to fit the meter of the line: Dark-clouded Zeus, Aegis-bearing Zeus, Father of gods and men, Son of Kronos,

Lord of lightning, etc. Achilles has some thirty-six different epithets. In the oral tradition, such formulae lend themselves easily to memorization and the singer has a ready-made phrase for each metrical situation so that he can compose his song as as he goes. These formulas indicate to scholars the certainty that the epics went through an oral stage; they testify to the plastic state of the epics before they come to be written down. The Greek epics were, indeed, a living poetry.

History of the Text   It is not certain how the present text differs from that known to Greek antiquity. The earliest known manuscript of Homer is that of the Marcian Library at Venice, placed there in the fifteenth century by Cardinal Bessarion, but the version we now have derives from copies of the poems made by scholars in Alexandria in the first two centuries of our era. Divergent texts seem to have been harmonized by the Alexandrines, and it is possible that they themselves divided the poem into twenty-four books (one for each letter of the Greek alphabet); some scholars feel, however, that this division may have been Homer's own, as each book is about the right length to have been sung in a single evening. The student interested in the history of the *Iliad*, from its first known presence to its first printing in 1488 by Demetrias Damilas of Florence, will want to consult J. A. Davison's "the Transmission of the Text," in Wace and Stubbings' *A Companion to Homer* (Oxford, 1963).

Causes of The Trojan War

Mythical   In the *Iliad* it is clear that Paris kidnapped Helen from her home in Sparta, but the great body of Greek mythology provides, as might be expected, a more involved account, laying all at the whim, caprice, and design of the gods.

The epic containing The Judgment of Paris is lost. We have, however, a summary of its plot, in a book by the Byzantine theologian and church father Photius (who lived from approximately 820 to 890 A.D.) called the *Myriobyblion* ("the library"). Even here we have a summary of a summary, for Photius is quoting another history of literature, the *Chrestomathy* of Proclus (who died late in the fifth century A.D.). The lost epic was called the *Kypria*, and was thought to be by Homer himself, though some ancient scholars speak of the *Kypria* as being by Stasinos or by Hegesias, about whose lives we know as much as we know about Homer's.

The plot of the *Kypria* is relatively simple: Themis (Natural Law) and Zeus decide that the earth is overpopulated. A great war is needed to thin out the number of men. The marriage of the mortal Peleus and the nymph Thetis (who will become the parents of Achilles) is chosen as the incident to provoke such a war. All the gods are invited to the wedding except Discord (the antithesis in concept of Themis or "order"). Discord is naturally offended, and seeks revenge. She secretly brings a golden apple to the wedding, inscribed "For the Fairest." Aphrodite, Pallas Athena, and Hera claim the apple. An impartial judge of their beauty is needed. Zeus chooses one of Priam's sons, Paris Alexandros, who has been sent away from Troy to live the life of a shepherd, as the oracle said at his birth that he would cause trouble for the city. He herds cattle on Mount Ida. Hermes tells him that he must judge among the three goddesses, and award the golden apple to the one he thinks most beautiful. Before he can judge, however, he is approached by each of the goddesses with a bribe. Pallas offers him wisdom; Hera offers him power; and Aphrodite offers him Helen of Sparta, the most beautiful of mortals. The young shepherd, banished from the life of the court, accepts Aphrodite's bribe and awards her the apple.

Hera and Pallas Athena are insulted, and become implacable foes of Troy; Aphrodite, meanwhile, whisks Helen away to that city from her husband Menelaos. Menelaos asks his brother Agamemnon for help, and together they organize a pan-Hellenic army to retrieve Helen from the Trojans.

The epic then tells of the setting out for Troy, with attendant adventures: the sacrifice of Agamemnon's daughter Iphigeneia for a good sailing wind, the abandoning of the wounded Philoktetes (as later employed as dramatic materials by Aeschylus and Sophocles). The rest of the epic apparently consists of battle scenes. It ends with Zeus' decision to make the fighting more even by withdrawing Achilles from the fighting; in the *Iliad*, "this is where we came in."

Historical   Because history no longer doubts that there was a Troy or a Trojan War, it is by no means implausible that a Greek expedition might have destroyed the city because of the rape of a Spartan woman. Most, however, subscribe to the more practical theory that the war was an economic one, and that the contention was over rights concerning trade routes. The riches uncovered on the archeological site of Troy are out of all proportion to the opportunities of its citizens to accumulate such wealth. It is therefore assumed that the Trojans controlled the shipping that passed through the Hellespont, as well as the overland trade routes that connected Greece and the Orient. The immense wealth of the Trojans can be accounted for if we suppose that they levied tolls and taxes on both land and sea trade. The Trojan war then would have been a Greek attempt to crush a Trojan monopoly. Or it could have been an open assault on a rich city which a Greek federation wanted for its own.

Names in Homer

The spellings in this volume follow, in great part, those of the Greek: for example, *Hektor* and *Menelaos* instead of the Latin *Hector* and *Menelaus*. In the eighteenth and nineteenth centuries, Latin was studied more than Greek, and most Greek literature was approached from a Latin point of view. Hence the traditional predilection for the Latin names of the gods: *Minerva* rather than *Pallas Athena*, *Mercury* rather than *Hermes*, etc. It is rapidly becoming the style among translators to render the names of Homer's characters as faithfully as possible to their appearance in the original Greek, but, we shall probably always say *Homer* and not the *Homeros* to which he would have responded. In addition, it is difficult to be both consistent and clear in rendering the Greek into English; thus words such as *Aeschylus* and *Mycenae*, *Achilles* (for *Akhilleus*), which are familiar to us in the Latinized form, have been retained. The following chart clarifies transliterations and their different equivalents (difficult pronunciations are indicated in parentheses with stressed syllables and long vowels indicated).

Greek	Traditional English	Latin
Aias (*eye-as*)	Ajax	Ajax
Alexandros	Alexander	Alexander
Andromakhe (*An-droma-ke*)	Andromache	Andromache
Aphrodite (*Af-ro-di-te*)	Aphrodite	Venus
Ares	Ares	Mars

Greek	Traditional English	Latin
Artemis	Artemis	Diana
(Pallas) Athena	Athene	Minerva
Demeter	Demeter	Ceres
Eos (*A-os*)	Dawn	Aurora
Hekabe (*Hek-a-be*)	Hecuba	Hecuba
Hektor	Hector	Hector
Helen	Helen	Helena
Hellas	Greece	Graecia
Hephaistos (*Hef-eyes-tos*)	Hephaestus	Vulcan
Hera (*Here-a*)	Hera	Juno
Hermes	Hermes	Mercury
Ilion	Troy	Ilium
Menelaos (*Men-e-la-os*)	Menelaus	Menelaus
Patroklos	Patroclus	Patroclus
Poseidon	Poseidon	Neptune
Skamandros	Scamander	Scamander
Teukros (*Tew-kros*)	Teucer	Teucer
Zeus (*Zews*)	Zeus	Jupiter

It is important, also, to understand that the Greeks of Homer's poetry had one name only, to which might be added (or substituted) the patronymic form (one's father's name with a special ending). Thus, *Odysseus Laertides* simply means *Odysseus, son of Laertes; Achilles Peliades* translates as *Achilles, son of Peleus.* And Greek names were frequently like those in Dickens: they tell something of the man's character. Odysseus means "The Wrathful"; he was so named by his grandfather Autolykos ("Wolf"). Hektor literally means "Mainstay." Interesting meanings, as they turn up, are noted in the "Commentary" through the COMPREHENSIVE SUMMARY, below.

The word *Greek* itself is taken from a Latin form; the Greeks of Homer's epic called themselves by various names: Argives (people of the Plain of Argos), Achaeans, Danaans, or Hellenes (contemporary Greece still calls itself Hellas). In the *Iliad*, the term *panhellene* would indicate that all the divergent tribes and small nations spoke dialects of the same language and had the beginnings of a national identity. We now refer to Homer's people as the Mycenaeans, as the past decade has uncovered vast remains of Homer's world, thought formerly to be mythological.

CAPSULE SUMMARY

The *Iliad* is built upon the plot of two angry and stubborn contentions: one is the war between the Greeks and the Trojans; the other, a private quarrel between the leader of the Greeks, Agamemnon Atreides (that is, son of Atreus), and the champion Greek warrior, Achilles Peleides.

The poem begins in the last year of the ten-year Trojan War. The conflict had begun when a punitive expedition of some 140,000 Hellenic warriors, under the command of Agamemnon of Mycenae of the Gold (in the plain of Argos), sailed to Troy in Asia Minor. Alexandros (or Paris), a prince of Troy, had abducted the wife of Agamemnon's brother Menelaos, and the Greek force was determined to retrieve her.

The opening describes a recent Greek raid on an outlying city for supplies, treasure, and captives. Agamemnon has captured the daughter of a priest of Apollo. The father offers a ransom and Agamemnon refuses. The priest and father then has Apollo send a plague among the Greeks and the daughter is returned. To replace his own loss, Agamemnon then takes a captive girl that Achilles had claimed for himself.

Achilles sulks, refuses to fight for the Greek cause and also withdraws his personal Myrmidon army—a serious loss to Greek power. In humiliation, Achilles begs his goddess-mother Thetis to have Zeus bring disgrace upon Agamemnon. A series of military setbacks then drives the Greeks from the Trojan walls and back against their ships, to which the Trojans are about to set fire. Achilles' companion, Patroklos, then comes to the aid of the Greeks, wearing Achilles' armor to give them new spirit. He drives the Trojans back to their city, but is then killed by Hektor, chief of the Trojan warriors.

Achilles enters the battle again, to avenge himself of Patroklos' death. He slays Hektor, desecrates his body and drags it around and around the walls of the city, then to the Greek camp where he allows it to lie neglected and dishonored. Patroklos' body, at the same time, is given a hero's funeral.

Priam, king of Troy and father of Hektor, comes alone to the Greek camp to beg for Hektor's body. So tragic is the plea that Achilles complies and Hektor is buried honorably in Troy.

COMPREHENSIVE SUMMARY

Book I: The Book of The Quarrel

The epic begins with the lesser, personal contention between Achilles and Agamemnon. In a raid on part of the
Troad (the name of the large district of which Troy is the
chief city) the Greeks have captured a girl named Khryseis,
the daughter of a priest of Apollo, Khryses. It is Agamemnon's in-
tention to keep the girl as a slave and concubine, and to take
her home with him to Mycenae in Argos (central Greece) as
part of his booty. (A warrior's honor, as we shall see throughout the poem, is enhanced not only by his prowess in battle
but also by the plunder and number of slaves he carries away.)

Khryses comes to the Greek ships, beached on the shore
across a wide plain from Troy, to beg Agamemnon to accept
a ransom for his daughter. The Greek refuses. Khryses therefore
asks Apollo to punish Agamemnon and his company. Apollo
rains the Greek camp with arrows bearing the plague, shooting
first the mules and hunting dogs, and then the men.

COMMENTARY: We are to imagine that the arrows are super-
                   natural, though, characteristically, the shooting
of them is described with intense realism; Homer imi-
tates the twanging snap of Apollo's silver bow and the
quivering of the bowstring:

        e klangsan d'ar o-i-stoy ep omon khomen-oy-o (46)
            (arrows clanged in the quiver on his shoulder)
        dana de klang-ga genet argire-oy-o bi-oy-o (49)
            (terrifying, the twang of that silver bow)

        Apollo, whom we know in later myth as a god
of light and healing, is here a local deity, Apollo Smintheus ("Apollo Red Mouse"), a god far more primitive
and tribal than the Apollo of classical times. The Greeks
at this time burned their dead, and Homer evokes a
scene of pity and suffering by noting that the funeral fires
burned all day and all night.

Fire, as will be seen, is the dominant image of the *Iliad*; practically every element of the poem is in some way connected with fire—Homer's symbol of the violence and waste of war.

For nine days Apollo shoots the plague arrows. On the tenth, Hera, mother of the gods and wife of the supreme Zeus, tells Achilles to call an assembly, at which he suggests to Agamemnon that they consult a priest as to the cause of the plague. (A priest was "a prophet, a. dream interpreter," a man who translated the signs given by the gods to mankind.) Kalkhas, the bird-interpreter, explains that Apollo is angry with the Greeks because Agamemnon had refused to accept Khryses' ransom for his daughter.

Agamemnon agrees to give the girl back, but will take Achilles' female prize, Briseis, instead. Achilles is furious, naturally, and there ensues the first of the bitter quarrels staged throughout the poem.

COMMENTARY: The quarrel characterizes both men. Agamemnon, for all his greatness as king and military commander, is revealed as a jealous, greedy, and selfish man. His actions are clearly presented as childish and indefensible. The reader must realize, however, that the structure of Greek society allowed such petulance; in a nation of heroes, personal honor determined social stature, and a great part of such honor was, in times of war, represented by the spoils of victory. Achilles is short-tempered and headstrong, yet Agamemnon is no less stubborn than he. The irony of this quarrel, then, must not be missed: the two chief warriors argue bitterly over the possession of a girl who belongs to neither of them even while they are in the midst of a cruel war over the possession of another woman, Helen.

The quarrel grows to such a pitch that Pallas Athena has to step in to keep Achilles from killing Agamemnon. Then old Nestor, the sage and senior warrior (a peacemaker throughout the poem) intervenes and offers both a compromise and a fatherly rebuke. He makes a pointed speech on violence, and advises Achilles to defer to Agamemnon, his chief, and for Agamemnon to drop his anger at Achilles, the best of the Greek fighters.

Achilles, however, stalks away in sullen anger. He *has* deferred to Agamemnon and will give up his prize girl but he will not fight again for the Greeks. Agamemnon has (in his own eyes) saved his honor but he has lost the cooperation of the best of his fighters.

Agamemnon sends Odysseus, the cleverest and slyest of of the Greeks, to return Khryseis to her father Khryses; and sends the heralds (or messengers) Talthybios and Eurybates to bring back Briseis with them from Achilles' headquarters.

Achilles meanwhile has gone to the sea to weep at his bad luck and humiliation. His immortal mother, the sea-nymph Thetis, hears him and comes from the ocean to comfort him. Achilles remembers that Thetis once saved Zeus himself from disgrace by calling in the hundred-armed Briareus, and begs her to implore Zeus to have the Trojans drive the Greeks into the sea.

Thetis promises that she will plead his case before the father of gods and men, and does. Zeus agrees to give Achilles honor greater than that of all other men. It is known to these immortals that Achilles' fate is to have a short but glorious life, but the terms of his glory have not yet been worked out. Zeus consents to give Achilles revenge upon the rest of the Greeks at the expense of angering Hera, whose heart is with the Argive forces and against the Trojans. Zeus' consent (lines 528-530) has always been admired as one of the great passages in Homer:

> The son of Kronos spoke, and nodded his dark brow,
> The godly hair of the ruler flowed down from his immortal head,
> And great Olympos shook.

Hera and Zeus squabble, until Zeus threatens her with physical violence. The quarrel ends badly for Hera. Her son, the lame smith and architect of the gods, Hephaistos, god of fire, comforts her, and reminds her that (as he well knew, having once been tossed off Olympos) one cannot withstand Zeus. The first book ends with the gods being served nectar (the gods' magic drink, as ambrosia was their magic food and ointment) by Hephaistos, whose limping causes them all to laugh. The last line of the book shows us Zeus and Hera sleeping peacefully beside each other.

COMMENTARY: Note that the book has a well balanced symmetry: it opens with the imperfections of humankind and closes with a picture of the perfect life of the gods. The gods are aloof, ultimately untroubled by the unevenness of existence. Their quarrels end in harmony; imperfection to them is something to laugh at. Human disharmony, on the other hand, is difficult to mend. The action of the first book has split the command of the Greek armies. The peacemaker Nestor, who smoothed over the anger of Achilles and Agamemnon, can never be as effective as Hephaistos. Thus, at the outset, Homer sets up the great contrast between the life of men and the life of gods that will be one of the strong themes of the epic.

All the art of Homer's time tended to be built symmetrically. Note the way in which Homer has balanced matters in the first book: the funeral pyres of the plague victims and the sacrificial burning of the hundred oxen that Agamemnon sends to Khryses to propitiate Apollo; the two prize girls, Khryseis and Briseis; the anger of Agamemnon and the anger of Achilles repeated in the anger of Hera and Zeus; the supplication of Khryses and the supplication of Thetis (both bringing trouble to the Greeks).

Homer begins his epics *in medias res,* as the Roman poet Horace said ("in the middle of the plot"). It would be just as well to say that he begins toward the end. All but the final sweep of action is left to happen in both the *Iliad* and the *Odyssey.* Homer fills in what went before as he progresses—and fills in a lot more, so that what seems to be a narrow scope for an epic (the plain before Troy and Troy itself) turns out to be the focus for hundreds of details—biographies, myths, geography, history—which will be woven into the fabric of the main action.

Book II: The Book of the Armies

The first half of Book II is a picture of complex treachery and chaos. Zeus has sent a false dream to Agamemnon (complying with Thetis' request that he bring the Greeks to confusion and defeat), leading Agamemnon to believe that Hera has decided in favor of the Greeks and that they are to win the war immediately. Agamemnon believes the dream (though Nestor has his suspicions), but his strategy is devious indeed. He tells the army that they are to leave Troy and return to their homes. He knows that his leaders will not allow this, and that their inciting the men to stay and fight is just the thing needed at the moment to move them into battle. So the effort of Odysseus and the other leaders to turn the men toward Troy rather than the ships is an unwitting deceit, for the dream was false.

COMMENTARY: The principal impact of these scenes of orders and counterorders is one of confusion and misdirection. Homer dramatizes powerfully the problems of an army with many leaders, and of a time when no man knows what the gods have in store. Dreams, like oracles, must be interpreted, and interpretation is never certain.

Note the complexities of the confusion:

1. Agamemnon is miscounseled by an evil dream sent from Zeus.
2. The advice of the dream is passed on to the chiefs (but not to the men).
3. Agamemnon proceeds to send the men home to Greece, acting exactly opposite to the dream's counsel.
4. Hera sends Pallas Athena to countermand Agamemnon's orders; Pallas sends Odysseus to take over the command of the Argive forces. He carries Agamemnon's scepter (the symbol of command) and marshals the army.
5. Thersites, a chronic complainer, scolds Agamemnon for miscommand, and is rebuked and beaten by Odysseus. This scene show clearly the moral confusion and chaos in which the Greek forces find themselves.
6. Then Odysseus and Nestor interpret signs that they say are indicative of good fortune for the Greeks. Odysseus remembers the snake that ate the nine sparrows and was turned to stone—which he interprets as the nine years of fighting, after which Troy (the snake) will be defeated— and Nestor remembers the "lightning on the right" (a good omen) when they set out for Troy. He also suggests that Agamemnon should review the troops.

7. Agamemnon, in another about-face, approves of these speeches, calls another council of leaders, and prepares to launch a major offensive against Troy.

In the second half of the book, the men are finally marshaled and march across the meadows of the river Skamandros (a powerful and grand image, with the gleam of the bronze armor and weapons flashing into the sky, so that the sky seems to be on fire), Homer gives a catalogue of the tribes of both armies. This charming list is far more than mere statistics. Homer has woven into it a geography of his peoples, many genealogies, even myths and bits of local history. In giving us a record of the "lords of the ships and the number of the ships" Homer has in effect constructed a vast panorama of Greece and the Troad.

The Argive Expedition

People of	Leaders	Number of Ships
Boiotia	Leitos and Peneleos	50
Aspledon, Orkhomenos	Askalaphos, Ialmenos	30
Phokis	Skhedios, Epistrophos	40
Lokris	Aias, son of Oileus	40
Euboia	Elephenor	40
Athens	Menestheus	50
Salamis	Aias, son of Telemon	12
Argos and Tiryns	Diomedes, Euryalos, and Sthenelos	80
Mycenai	Agamemnon	100
Lacedaimon	Menelaos	60
Pylos	Nestor	90
Arkadia	Agapenor	60
Bouprasion and Elis	Thalpios (10 ships) Amphimakhos (10) Diores (10) Polyzeinos (10)	40
Doulikhion	Meges	40
Kephallenia, Ithaka, and Zakynthos	Odysseus	12
Aitolia	Thoas	40
Crete	Idomeneus	80
Rhodes	Tlepolemos	9

People of	Leaders	Number of Ships
Syme	Nireus	3
Nisyros and other islands	Pheidippos and Antiphos	30
Pelasgian Argos (confederation of Hellenes, Myrmidons, and Achaeans)	Achilles	50
Phylake and Pyrasos	Podarkes	40
Pherai	Eumelos	11
Thaumakia and Methone	Medon (lieutenant for Philoktetes)	7
Trikke, Ithome, and Oichalia	Podaleirios and Makhaon	30
Ormenios	Eurypylos	40
Argissa	Polypoites	40
Kyphos	Gouneus	22
Magnesia	Prothoös	40

The Trojan Confederacy

People of	Leaders
Troy	Hektor
Dardania	Aeneas, Arkhelokhos, and Akamas
Zeleia	Pandaros
Adresteia	Adrestos and Amphios
Perkote and Praktion	Asios
Larissa	Hippothoös, Pylaios
Thrace	Akamas and Peiroös
Thrace: Kikonians	Euphemos
Amydon: Paionians	Pyraikhmes
Paphlagonia	Pylaimones
Alybe: Halizones	Odios and Epistrophos
Mysia	Khromis and Ennomos
Phrygia	Phorkys and Askanios
Maionia (Lydia)	Mesthles and Antiphos
Karia	Nastes and Amphimakhos
Lycia	Sarpedon and Glaukos

Between the two heroic catalogues of men, ships, and
countries Homer introduces our first view of Troy. Iris (the

rainbow) has come to warn the Trojans that the Greeks are marching in full strength against them, in what appears to be a major attack. Hektor, the chief of the Trojan forces, rallies his troops at a hill outside Troy called Batieia (The Wooded Hill). The area is known to the gods as The Barrow of the Leaping Myrinna. For the moment the gods are with Troy, and the air is ominous with signs of a Greek defeat. Agamemnon, Nestor, Idomeneus (leader of the Cretans), the two Aiantes (plural of Aias; that is, Aias the larger, son of Telamon, and Aias the smaller, son of Oileus), Diomedes, Odysseus and Menelaos (who makes his entry into the poem at this point) sacrifice to Zeus and pray for victory, but Zeus does not listen to the prayer.

COMMENTARY: This entire book is the first evil fruit of Agamemnon's offense to Achilles. Homer is working from the ancient concept that a man who cannot control his own passions cannot control other men. Agamemnon has a blemish in his character—a tragic flaw that, with luck, could have been inconsequential, but, like all flaws, bears within it the potential for disaster. Homer begins his story just when that blemish—stubborn arrogance—has, through a chain of events, brought confusion to the entire Greek army.

    The second book is one of soldiery and soldiering; it is a book of sudden preparations in one direction, abruptly to be changed to sudden preparations in another. From end to end it is a picture of shouting, impetuous men, and finally of men marching, "white with dust, like threshers on the threshing floor," and of men scurrying to arms to defend a city.

Book III: The Book of The Duel Between Paris and Menelaos

The book opens with the two armies facing each other on the plain outside Troy. The Trojans are shouting like cranes (their battle cry) but the Greeks are silent and grim.

Paris (Alexandros) steps from the Trojan ranks and challenges any Greek to fight him. The challenge is accepted by Menelaos. The two lovers of Helen face each other between the armies. But Paris was not counting on Menelaos coming forward and at first flinches, "like a man who has stepped on a snake."

Paris proposes that they fight for possession of Helen, if the kings will accept their duel as a token war. The winner is to keep Helen without further argument, and the war will be over, whoever wins. This is acceptable, and sacrificial animals are sent for, to bind the oath before the gods. It is a magnificent solution to the terrible war, and both sides are happy to accept the terms.

Iris, meanwhile, has told Helen what is about to happen. We first see Helen at the loom, like any honest Greek housewife. She is embroidering pictures of the two armies fighting over her. She hastens to the Skaian Gate, where many citizens are standing on the wall, watching the two armies in the field.

Here Homer stages a great scene, for Helen is rarely seen by the people, and she is as much a rarity as the sight of the armies. The old men of the city marvel at her beauty, and mutter that indeed she is a woman as beautiful as a goddess but that she ought to be sent "back to the ships," for her presence is a threat to the city's security.

Priam, Helen's father-in-law, treats her as a loved daughter, and asks her to identify the Greek warriors they can see in the front ranks. She identifies Agamemnon, Odysseus, Aias, and Idomeneus. Helen scans the lines for her brothers Kastor and Polydeukes, not realizing that they have been long dead.

COMMENTARY: Homer catches here the psychology of the war. Helen's kinsmen have been outside the walls of her city for nine years, and yet she has not learned from them the news of her family. Nor have they seen her all that while.

Priam then rides out to officiate at the oath. But once the oath is made, Priam has no heart to watch the duel, and returns to the Trojan walls.

The duel is a surprise. Paris and Menelaos fight; Menelaos' sword breaks, but he drags Paris by the helmet back into the Greek lines. At this point the goddess Aphrodite comes down and takes Paris away to his own bed.

While the Greeks are in consternation at this super-natural turn of affairs, Aphrodite goes to Helen on the wall and tells her that Paris is waiting for her in their bedroom. The introduction of so crassly erotic a situation at such a tense time is unseemly even to Helen, and she rebukes Aphrodite and refuses to go. Aphrodite has her way, however, being a god-dess, and Helen goes to Paris, telling him that she wishes he had died on the battlefield.

COMMENTARY: Homer's picturing of Helen is always as a wom-an indecisive, double-minded, a bit childish, and both seductive and waspish. Her confusion is under-standable. She has just seen her husband for the first time in nine years, and she is willing to go back to him. At the same time she is unwilling to give up Paris. Aphrodite has never been mistaken for the goddess of reason.

Meanwhile, the Trojans are so ashamed of Paris (whom they imagine to have escaped as a coward) that they help Menelaos hunt for him in their ranks.

Agamemnon declares that Menelaos is the victor, by default, demands the return of Helen forthwith, and is cheered by the Greek army.

COMMENTARY: The design of Book III is simple and direct. It has two clear lines of narration that weave across each other: the duel between Paris and Menelaos, and the figure of Helen. The dark confusion of the pre-ceding book clarifies into a crystal certainty when Paris proposes that the war be limited to a single duel. But the book progresses toward uncertainty all over again. Aphrodite could not have done worse than spirit away Paris, for by doing so she opens the way to the breaking of the oath (which happens in the next book), plunging the two armies back into war; and she undermines the character of Paris.

Paris bears the unmanly burden of being beautiful and to his heroically masculine brother Hektor he is a "strange man." He is uncertain of himself (as we see when he recoils from Menelaos at the beginning of the duel), and he feels the guilt of being the operative cause

of the war. But his real burden is made clear in the bedroom scene: he, like Helen, is under the spell of Aphrodite, caught in the magic of sex. Later (in Book VI)
Helen discloses something of the ambiguity of her love
affair with Paris by saying helplessly that perhaps her
and Paris' frivolous romance will at least be something
for poets to make poems of.

We see that both Paris and Helen are trapped
in their own characters: they are lovers and nothing else.
Aphrodite will not let Paris be a warrior (to Helen's
shame) and will not let Helen be a normal woman.

The book ends in terrible irony. The rejoicing is
a false happiness. All that remains is to see by what means
the imperfections of human nature or the malice of the
gods plunge the two sides back into war.

Note that the book begins with shouting Trojans
and silent Greeks, and ends with shouting Greeks and
silent Trojans. It is organized around two madnesses rec-
ognized in Greek psychology: the madness of sexual
desire and the madness of slaughter in battle. Both are
possessions, as by a demon, both "enthusiasms" (a Greek
word that means cataleptic, having been seized by a
god). As the book ends, Paris has the one madness, Menelaos the other. And caught between them, a symbol of
all the agony of the war, is the beautiful Helen, disciple
of Aphrodite, from whose cunning even Zeus is not free.

Book IV: The Book of The Broken Truce

The gods, drinking nectar served them by Hebe, goddess
of youth, look down on Troy. They watch the action of the
preceding book, the unfinished duel of Menelaos and Paris. To
Zeus' mind, as to Agamemnon's, Menelaos is the victor. Zeus
says that the war has reached a crisis: it can fall either toward
peace, "and the city of King Priam can be a place fit for men
to live in, and Menelaos can carry away with him Helen of the
Argives." Or the violence can begin all over again.

Zeus is in effect making a plea for neutrality on the part
of the gods. He loves Troy above all other cities of men, for
it has never failed to honor him with sacrifices. Hera and Pallas
Athena, however, are determined to see Troy brought down.

Zeus in his short-tempered anger accuses Hera of wanting to go through Troy's streets and eat all the people alive.

Zeus' love of the Trojans is mere favoritism to Hera. She names her own favorite cities: Argos, Sparta, and Mycenae, and says that he may destroy them whenever he wishes. They compromise, deciding to bring havoc to both sides, and Zeus stipulates that Troy must break the oath that Priam and Agamemnon have just made.

Pallas Athena goes down, disguising herself as the warrior Laodokos (a name that means, ironically, "counselor to the people"), and advises Pandaros that he can win honor and renown by shooting Menelaos, who imagines that there is a truce and that he can move freely between the armies without being on his guard.

Pandaros shoots, and Pallas guides the arrow so that it only grazes Menelaos, yet draws enough blood to show all onlookers that Menelaos came within a hair's breadth of being killed.

The effect is just as Pallas wished. The Greeks, who had taken off their armor as a symbol of the truce, hastily re-arm. Agamemnon marshals the troops to continue the attack that was postponed by Paris' offer. The doctor Makhaon heals Menelaos. Agamemnon moves among his captains—Idomeneus, Aias, Nestor, Diomedes, and Odysseus—inciting them to bravery (principally by innuendo and insult). He plans to move all the troops in phalanx—a close, even battle line.

The Greeks attack furiously, and the gods Terror, Fear, and Hate are among them. The Trojans fall back in dismay at the fury and relentlessness of the attack, crying aloud. Two kinds of screams fill the air—triumphant battle cries and men crying with pain.

Apollo incites the Trojans; Pallas, the Greeks. The book draws to a close with a fierce battle scene, and the last line describes dead Greeks and Trojans lying together in the dust.

COMMENTARY: In the *Iliad* it is the Greeks, not the Trojans, who are habitually treacherous. When Pandaros shoots Menelaos he is committing an act out of character with the city, and the shock is profound to both sides. Pandaros

is from the outlying country, and has come a long way
to fight on the Trojan side. He is the spirit of Asia, as
his use of the bow indicates. (The Greeks were spear
fighters; their swords were secondary weapons.) In one
sense the poem is always aware of the great difference
between Europe and Asia. Troy is an Asian city, but is
on the Mediterranean coast and has a European flavor
to it. Hektor, for instance, is as Greek as the Greeks. His
sense of honor and fair play would never have allowed
him to break the truce, particularly by shooting from
afar and without warning.

The critic Rachel Bespaloff (see the BIBLIOG-
RAPHY) feels that Helen symbolizes the contrast in the
poem between Europe and Asia, pointing out that Aphrodite, as Homer presents her, is more like the Asian goddess of love and fertility, Astarte, than the graceful
Aphrodite of later Greek religion. Helen is therefore a
symbol of the Greek character caught in the languid, sen-
sual spirit of Asia. Certainly if we compare Helen's home
in Sparta with the picture that Homer gives us of Troy,
the contrast is vivid. Troy is rich and opulent; its trade
is with Phoenicia and the Levantine; King Priam's fifty
sons and their wives and fifty daughters and their hus-
bands, all of whom sleep in a great palace with a hundred
bedrooms, belongs to the world of Baghdad and oriental
splendor that we associate with *The Arabian Nights*.
Sparta, on the other hand, is the very symbol even today
of strict military discipline and of the virtues of ab-
stinence, moral toughness, and simplicity.

This book begins with the hope of peace (a possi-
bility proposed by Zeus) and ends with a raging battle.
For the first time we see the descriptions of death in
battle for which Homer is famous. They are exactly described, almost from a medical point of view, and yet
they are told with pity and a tragic sense of the loss of
life. The descriptions are never anonymous, no matter
how insignificant the warriors. Nor does Homer take
sides; he is not a propagandist for the Greeks. His amaz-
ing detachment is like that of Zeus himself, who watches
with keen attention but feels the claims of both contenders.

Book V: The Book of Diomedes

The dominant figure of this book is the Greek Diomedes, son of Tydeus, on whom the battle madness falls. He is given *menos* (force, strength) and *tharsos* (courage) by Pallas Athena, so that he can have his *aristeia,* or moment of glory. The battle madness itself was a divine possession, and was spoken of as a kind of drunkenness.

First Diomedes kills Phegeus, one of the two sons of Dares (the other son, Idaios, is saved by Hephaistos, god of fire). Before the battle becomes full-scale, Pallas Athena slyly leads away Ares, the god of war, on the grounds that neither he nor she should anger Zeus by taking part in the fighting. This neutrality, as we shall see, will come to nothing, and the gods will figure in the battle.

There follow fifty lines of battle description in which we are told of the fighting of Agamemnon, Idomeneus, Menelaos, Meriones, Meyes, and Eurypylos before the story returns to Diomedes, who receives an arrow in the shoulder from the bow of Pandaros. Pallas, however, is quick to heal the wound. While she is treating Diomedes she urges him to stab Aphrodite, if he should see her in the battle, thus breaking the neutrality of the gods which Pallas Athena herself imposed.

Diomedes goes back into the fray "like a lion among sheep." He kills and kills. (Lines 145-165 give an account of the victims, relating who they are, and what kinds of tragedies their deaths cause in their families.)

Aeneas (who later will lead the Trojan survivors to Italy, where they will re-found Troy and call it Rome—the subject of Vergil's Latin epic *The Aeneid*) is distressed by Diomedes' slaughter of the Trojans. He seeks out Pandaros, whom he asks to shoot Diomedes with an arrow. Pandaros explains to Aeneas (together with an account of his journey to Troy, and of his family in Lycia) that he has already shot Diomedes, as well as Menelaos, to no avail. It may be, he thinks, that Diomedes is a god in disguise. Aeneas and Pandaros plan to attack Diomedes in close fighting, and ride toward him in their chariot. Diomedes has no fear of them; he and his companion Sthenelos are more interested in capturing Aeneas's horses, which are descended from the immortal horses given by Zeus to Tros in recompense for Zeus' abduction of Tros' son Ganymede, whom he made cupbearer to the gods.

Pandaros casts a spear and imagines that he has killed Diomedes. As he is rejoicing over his apparent victory, Diomedes, who is not hurt, transfixes Pandaros' face with a spear, killing him. Then he throws a rock and crushes Aeneas' hip.

Aeneas is the son of Ankhises and the goddess Aphrodite (his begetting is told in the "Hymn to Aphrodite" that was once thought to be by Homer), so Aphrodite, whose sympathies are strongly with the Trojans anyway, comes to save her son from Diomedes, who, in his battle madness, stabs her in the wrist. Apollo comes to her rescue, taking charge of the wounded Aeneas. Ares lends Aphrodite his chariot and she and Iris go immediately to Olympos, where Dione, Aphrodite's mother, heals her wound and comforts her by telling her of other occasions when the gods were wounded by mortals.

COMMENTARY: One of the sustained contrasts in the *Iliad* is the ultimately carefree life of the gods as contrasted to man's unhappiness. Life is easily comic to the immortals.

No sooner is Aphrodite on Olympos than Homer has her say (with typical womanly exaggeration) that Diomedes wants to stab Zeus. Dione treats Aphrodite as if she were a child who has stubbed her toe. Pallas Athena, with consummate cattiness, asks Aphrodite if her hand was cut by the brooch of some woman she was dragging from the Greeks to give to the Trojan men. Zeus steps in to rebuke Aphrodite (while tacitly approving of Pallas' tart remark), advising her to keep to her proper business, "the secret delights of the bed."

Meanwhile Apollo guards Aeneas. Diomedes tries thrice to wound Apollo, until he is warned away. Apollo takes Aeneas to his shrine at Pergamos, where Artemis, goddess of animals, hunting, and childbirth, and Leto, her mother, cure him. Apollo makes a phantom image of Aeneas and puts it in the battle in Aeneas' stead.

The battle is going badly for the Trojans, so Ares himself, the god of war, takes the shape of the warrior Akamas and joins the fighting. He incites the Trojans by urging them to rescue Aeneas.

While Ares stirs the Trojans to victory, Sarpedon, who has come from Lycia "far away" to be an ally, urges Hektor to harder fighting. He reminds him that the Greeks will not cease until they have burned the city and killed all the men, and that the delay on the part of the Trojans will be fatal.

The Greek battle line is unbroken, and steadily advances. In one of his most graphic similes Homer describes the dust and intensity of the Greek approach:

> As the wind sifts chaff above the sacred threshing place,
> When the winnowers are at work, so that blonde Demeter
> In the streaming wind divides the husk from the grain
> And the white chaff falls in a heap, so the Akhaians
> Whitened under the dust of their galloping horses
> That stirred dust high into the bronze-bright sky. (499-504)

COMMENTARY: The simile is not only graphically exact, helping Homer's audience to visualize what few of them had seen, a chariot and infantry charge, but is also pointedly ironic in that an image of peace is used to explain a scene of war.

Apollo, Ares, and Hate drive the Trojans against the Greeks, but the Greeks stand fast. Among the Greek casualities to whom Homer pays particular attention in this section are the brothers Orsilokhos and Krethon, sons of Diokles (of Phere in the Peloponnesos) who counts among his ancestors the river Alpheios. These two were raised "as two lions" in the Greek mountains, and they fall, when Aeneas kills them, like two pine trees felled in the forest. Menelaos, pitying them, goes out to recover their bodies, helped by Nestor's son, Antilokhos. Aeneas stands firm, at first, and it looks as if there's to be a duel, but Aeneas backs away.

Diomedes recognizes Ares among the Trojans, and orders the Greeks to hold their line but to move back while fighting. The Trojans now have the offensive.

Tlepolemos, son of Herakles, meets Sarpedon, and they exchange insults before they fight. Sarpedon is wounded but Tlepolemos is killed. The battle rages on. Odysseus kills seven men. Hektor and Ares, fighting side by side, slaughter Greeks as fast as they can hurl their spears. As the Greeks are thrown into confusion and retreat, Hera herself comes down (disguised as Stentor, whose voice was as loud as that of fifty men) and urges the Greeks to harder fighting. Pallas Athena comes down also and shares a chariot with Diomedes.

The book began with Diomedes' *aristeia,* and now it returns to it. Pallas and Diomedes attack Ares himself. Diomedes sticks him in the stomach with a spear, and Pallas pushes it in, then pulls it out again. Ares screams like nine thousand men. Both armies freeze with fear at the shout. Ares flees to Olympos, where he complains to Zeus that Athena has gone too far, inciting Diomedes to attack Ares himself. Zeus rebukes Ares, calling him a whining liar. "You are the most hateful of gods," he says. Just as Zeus, at the beginning of the previous book, praises peace and hopes that the war can be ended, here he deplores war altogether.

Hera and Pallas, having got Ares out of the battle, return to Olympos, happy with their success.

COMMENTARY: The design of this book is more rhythmic than geometric. It moves in waves, alternating scenes with a regular, fast rhythm. Homer, for symmetry's sake, repeats scenes with dramatic variations. Diomedes is wounded by Pandaros but eventually kills him; he is bested by Ares and, with Athena's help, eventually wounds the god. The impact of the book is one of raging violence and death. Diomedes is the book's central character, though we can see emerging, on the Trojan side the heroic figure of Hektor, who will loom larger and larger as the epic progresses.

Book VI: The Book of Hector and Andromakhe

The gods have left, but the battle rages on, filling the great level plain between the rivers Xanthos and Simoeis. Aias has his moment of glory, as does Diomedes again, and Euryalos and Polypoites. Menelaos takes the Trojan ally Adrastos alive, to be kept for ransom, but Agamemnon, feeling that nothing but the utmost cruelty will win the war, kills him. The Greeks have the upper hand, and begin another advance toward the city. Helenos the Trojan holds the offensive back, and sends his brother Hektor to the city to ask the women to supplicate Pallas Athena to help them overcome Diomedes.

While Hektor goes on his mission, the scene changes to

the battle's midst. Here Diomedes faces Glaukos, and offers to fight him if he is not a god. Glaukos replies with the famous line:

Glaukos replies with the famous line:

As the generations of leaves are the generations of men *(146)*

Glaukos goes on to tell of his ancestry, relating, in effect, the romance of Bellerophontes. Sisyphos, son of Aiolos the god of winds, lived in Argos and begat a son, Glaukos, who begat Bellerophontes. Bellerophontes, Glaukos tells, was falsely accused by King Proitos' queen of trying to seduce her and was sent to King Iobates, father of the queen, taking with him "many baneful and destructive signs written in a folded tablet" which Proitos gave him. (This is the only sure reference in Homer to writing. It appears from this passage that the art of writing was known in Homer's time, but was by no means a common skill.) Presumably, the message asks Iobates to kill Bellerophontes, and Iobates therefore sends Bellerophontes to kill the Chimaera (lion-headed, snake-tailed, and with a goat's body), feeling certain that the Chimaera will instead kill Bellerophontes. When Bellerophontes succeeds in this task, Iobates sends him to accomplish other impossible feats, sure that he will die in one of them. Finally the king realizes that Bellerophontes is descended from the gods, gives up trying to kill him, and gives him his daughter as a wife. One of his children was Hippolokhos, father of Glaukos, another Laodameia, mother of Sarpedon.

Diomedes remembers that his grandfather once had Bellerophontes as a guest, and that he himself inherited a golden cup that Bellerophontes had left as a memorial of the visit. It is not fitting that they fight; they swear friendship, and exchange armor, so that they will know each other in the battles. Homer notes, with something like a broad grin, that Glaukos is a fool to agree to the exchange, as he is wearing golden armor worth a hundred oxen, while Diomedes' armor is of bronze and worth only nine.

COMMENTARY: There are several reasons why this long story is placed here. *One*: it may well be an elaborate joke, a raucous soldier's tale of how Diomedes bilked the innocent Glaukos of his golden armor. Diomedes has just been prevented from stripping Aeneas of his armor by Ares. *Two*: it is one of the many myths inserted into the fabric of the narrative to broaden the scope of the work, emphasizing that an army is a collection of men who come from far away and bring with them the flavor and history of their native land. *Three*: it serves to balance the slaughterous madness of Diomedes, to show him as a man of good will when he is not "a lion among sheep."

The rest of the book is devoted to Hektor in Troy. When he reaches the Skaian Gate (the entrance to the city that faces the battle plain) he is surrounded by anxious wives and mothers who ask about their kin. He then goes to his mother Hekabe and his sister Laodike, instructing them to give a fine robe to Pallas Athena in the hope that she will keep Diomedes from the fighting. The women choose the finest of embroidered robes (Paris brought it from Phoenicia) and take it to Pallas' temple. Theano the priestess makes the prayer, but Pallas "turned her head away."

Hektor goes to the house of Paris and Helen, to urge Paris to return to battle. It is in this scene that our understanding of Helen is deepened, for it is clear that she is ashamed of the immense trouble she has caused. She talks with Hektor as to an understanding brother, and though Hektor came prepared to vent his anger, he is softened by both Paris and Helen. He agrees to meet Paris at the gates to return to the battlefield.

Hektor then goes in search of his wife Andromakhe and finds her on the city wall. She has their infant son with her, Skamandrios (named for the river that flows by Troy); he is also called Astyanax (Lord of the City). No more movingly human scene appears in Homer or other ancient literature. Hektor has a feeling that he is going to his death, and that his death will come (as it will) from Achilles, who killed his wife's father in the Theban war. Andromakhe tells Hektor that he is her father and mother, brother and husband, since he is her only kin left in the world. She therefore urges him to stay away from the battle. Hektor explains that if Troy is taken, she will become a slave and concubine to a Greek lord, and that he would rather die keeping that fate from her.

When they part he puts on his horse-tail helmet and bends to kiss his infant son, but the helmet frightens the child, who screams. He removes the helmet and "pitched the dear son playfully in his arms and kissed him." He then prays to Zeus to protect his son, and allow him to grow up and surpass his father as a hero.

Hektor assures Andromakhe that he is not going to be bested by any of the Greeks, but her fears are not quelled, and once he is gone she and her handmaidens weep for him as if he were already dead.

Paris and Hektor meet each other at the gates. Paris is described as a horse long pent up in his stall let out to frisk in the pasture. Hektor tells Paris that he must be more of a warrior, for the men talk about him behind his back. They go out to the battlefield talking of the day when there will be peace again, and the Greeks are driven away from their walls. Neither will live long enough to know that that day never comes.

COMMENTARY: This book falls into halves: the first is concerned with the battlefield; the second with Hektor in Troy with his mother, wife, and son. The theme of the book is fearful hope and expectancy, and, in this sense, is a tragic episode, for every hope in it will be frustrated. In one half of the book we have the myth of Bellerophontes, a romance in which a hero does impossible deeds and marries a princess and lives happily ever after. In the other half of the book we have the flesh-and-blood Hektor, whose life would be normal and sane except for the stubborn Greeks outside his walls, and who will die at their hands.

At the heart of the book is the supplication of Athena by the Trojan women, and her refusal (which they cannot know). This is the sign of Troy's doom that hangs as an invisible force over all the action in the book, even foolish Glaukos' giving up his golden armor to a wily Greek.

Book VII: The Book of The Greek Wall

Hektor and Paris return to the Trojan forces, and are "as welcome as a fair wind to sailors." Each goes immediately into battle; each kills a man and goes on to other fierce fighting. When Pallas perceives them, she comes down "like a flash." Apollo, who intends a Trojan victory, meets her and accuses her of wanting to see Troy defeated. They compromise for the moment by deciding to inspire Hektor to call a truce to permit single combat. The two armies sit. Pallas and Apollo take the form of vultures and sit in a tree, watching. Menelaos volunteers to meet Hektor. Agamemnon, however, dissuades him, pointing out that Hektor is stronger and will most certainly kill him.

Old Nestor then makes a speech in which he longs for his youth, and recounts some of the deeds of his own warrior days. He shames the Greeks into volunteering. Nine come forward: Agamemnon himself, Diomedes, the two Aiantes, Idomeneus and Idomeneus's comrade Meriones, Eurypylos, Thoas, and Odysseus. They draw lots to see who will take up the challenge.

The larger Aias, son of Telamon, is chosen. He arms and approaches Hektor with the boast that he is the bravest and strongest of the Greeks except Achilles, who is by his ships sulking because of the wrong done him by Agamemnon.

Hektor reminds Aias that he is no novice at fighting, and throws his spear. It sticks in Aias's bronze and ox-hide shield. Aias's spear penetrates Hektor's shield, body armor, and shirt beneath, but does not reach the flesh. They withdraw their spears and throw again; this time Hektor gets a superficial wound in the neck. They then throw rocks, crushing each other's shields. Just as they are drawing their swords for close combat, the heralds stop them, for night is coming on. They exchange gifts (a sword and sheath for Aias, a belt for Hektor).

In the Greek camp Nestor advises the building of a wall, to keep the Trojans from their part of the plain. It is to have a deep ditch before it, with wooden spikes set in it. The Greeks agree to this.

In Troy, Antenor speaks in assembly for that element of the Trojans who feel that they have broken their covenant with the Greeks (when Pandaros shot the arrow and canceled the truce) and that they ought, in all honor, to give Helen back, and thus stop the war. Paris refuses, though he is willing to give treasure instead. Idaios is chosen to go as an ambassador to the Greeks, to ask if they will accept treasure and if they will allow a brief truce for the burning of the dead. The Greeks refuse the former, grant the latter.

COMMENTARY: Idaios' speech to the Greeks is consciously comic, for he expresses the attitude of the common people, who wish that Helen had never been brought to Troy. He also wishes that Paris had lost his way somewhere far from Troy.

Both armies gather and cremate their dead in the night, and the Greeks begin building their earthen wall with the trench before it.

The book ends with a curious bit of business on Olympos, illustrating the implacable childishness of the gods, their jealousies, and their willingness to harrass mankind. Poseidon, god of the sea, complains to Zeus that the wall has been built without due sacrifice to the gods, and that the Greeks ought to be punished. Zeus, who is the voice of balanced reason among the gods, suggests ironically that the wall be torn down by Poseidon—after the war! Zeus nevertheless sends lightning flashes while the Greeks are banqueting (a supply ship has just put in from the island of Lemnos, with meats and wine).

COMMENTARY: This book recounts what the war must have been like for its first nine years: setbacks, duels to the draw, new plans, the laying of strategies, the problem of supplies, indecision, and the interference of the gods. This is a transitional book, closing the furious battle of the two preceding ones, and laying the groundwork for action to come. Its theme is the stubbornness that shields the causes of the war from rational settlement, either among the Trojans or between Trojan and Greek. It is clear that nothing will satisfy the Trojans but to drive the Greeks utterly away from the city, and nothing will satisfy the Greeks but to reclaim Helen, loot Troy, and burn it to the ground.

Book VIII: The Book of The Greek Entrapment

On Olympos Zeus calls the gods together and forbids them to interfere further in the war, on pain of being thrown into Tartaros, the deepest underworld which is as far below Hades as the earth is from the sky. To illustrate his strength, Zeus reminds the other gods that he is stronger than all of them together, and that if he were on one end of a golden cord let down from Olympos, and they on the other end on the earth, he could pull them all up and the earth and the sea with them. The gods are astounded and chagrined at this harsh command, and they are all silent except Athena, who points out that the gods can still *counsel* mortals.

Zeus then gets in his chariot, dressed in gold, and streams through the air to his sanctuary on Mount Ida, where he sits and watches the course of the war.

At dawn in Troy both armies move into battle. Zeus weighs the fates of the two armies on his scales. Because the Greeks are winning, he gives the advantage to the Trojans, sending lightning bolts to frighten the Greeks. In the rout, Nestor gets into trouble when Paris shoots his chariot horse in the head. Diomedes rescues Nestor, shooting Hektor's charioteer in the process.

But Hektor sees that the luck is running his way and with a new charioteer sets upon the retreating Greeks and drives them into confusion. Homer describes him as a newly inspired and raging warrior. He storms about in his chariot, taunting the Greeks, threatening to burn their ships, and hoping to get possession of Nestor's shield and Diomedes' armor, two of the most coveted prizes. He shouts encouragement to his four horses, Xanthos, Podargos, Aithon, and Lampos (Yellow, Flashfoot, Fire, and Torch). Hektor's *aristeia* begins to pose such a threat to the Greeks that Hera (herself afraid to go against Zeus's command) tries to talk Poseidon into stopping the Trojans, but he will not disobey Zeus.

Hektor drives the Greeks to their ships, and Agamemnon sees that if Hektor succeeds in firing the ships, they are indeed lost. Agamemnon prays to Zeus, who sends an eagle with a fawn in its talons as a sign that the Greeks are being protected. The Greeks therefore launch a counter-attack. Teukros, companion of Aias, has his wild hour of glory with his bow, shooting from behind Aias' large shield. He kills Trojan after Trojan, and his ambition is to kill Hektor. When he misses Hektor and brings down Priam's son Gorgythion, Homer describes the death in a simile that has always been one of the most famous passages in the poem:

> His limp neck bent to his shoulder as a poppy in a garden
>   leans
> Heavy with spring rain and the weight of its blossom (306-307)

But as Teukros is drawing his bow for another shot, Hektor heaves a rock at him and breaks his shoulder.

Fight as hard as they will, the Greeks cannot withstand Hektor, for the battle madness is on him. He has the staring eyes of a Gorgon, the weird sisters whose glance turned men to stone. He is also compared to Ares, and to a hound snapping at the hind feet of a wild boar.

Pallas Athena and Hera can no longer contain their anxiety, and arm themselves to come down and help the Greeks. Zeus, however, perceives them from Mount Ida, and sends Iris to warn them that unless they turn back he will burn them both with a stroke of lightning and that it will take ten years for their burns to heal. They turn back.

Zeus then returns to Olympos, calls the gods together (though Hera and Pallas are no longer on speaking terms with him, and sit apart, sulking), and tells them that the Greek fortunes will not change until Achilles relents and joins the fighting.

Night falls at Troy. Hektor decides to keep his forces outside the walls for the first time in the history of the war. His plan is to keep the Greeks penned all night, and to burn their ships in the morning. All the Trojans and their allies are marshaled in the camp, fifty thousand men. Old men and boys guard the city, and all wives keep fires burning, so that Greeks can't make a sneak attack there. Fifty watchfires burn in the Trojan camp. Here Hektor makes a boastful speech (and even wishes that he might be immortal and eternally young, if all of life could be as triumphant as he now feels it to be). This speech matches that of Zeus at the beginning of the book.

They sacrifice to the gods, but the gods refuse their prayers. A dramatic irony controls the situation: the Trojans have the upper hand by sheer strength and daring. The gods are against them. The Trojans are ignorant of this, however; their "hearts are high" and they have the Greeks at their mercy.

COMMENTARY: The symbolism of fire becomes more radiant: Zeus' lightning with which he threatens Pallas and Hera; Hektor's fire with which he threatens the Greek ships.

The theme of this book is the power of authority (as distinct from the military force of the warriors and the persuasive force of personality), and Homer consciously lays down a parallel between Zeus and Hektor. Both create new order by asserting power that was always theirs but which they had not used. The organized Trojan forces now stand in sharp contrast to the Greek, whose command is as disorganized as before and whose army, because of Achilles' anger, is crippled in its striking power.

The thousand fires that burn ominously through the night end the book with a sinister image, for these are the fires that can kindle the Greek ships.

Book IX: The Book of Achilles' Refusal

The Greeks are now trapped behind their defenses, waiting for the Trojan attack. They are desperately afraid: Homer compares their panic to a sudden storm at sea. This water imagery is continued in the comparison of Agamemnon's troubled heart to a "spring of dark water," and the image is made concrete in the tears of frustration that he weeps before his assembled chiefs.

COMMENTARY: The spring is a constant image in Greek poetry. Poetic inspiration came from a crystal-clear spring, *Kastalia,* and all fresh water (rain, springs, rivers) was considered sacred—a concept easily understood when we know that Greece is a dry, rocky country where most of the rivers dry up completely in the summer. The "spring of dark water" to which Agamemnon's tears are compared is brackish, evil water.

Agamemnon feels that Zeus is against him and the Greeks, and proposes that they return to Greece in dishonor. Diomedes refuses, saying that Agamemnon has the gift of power and command, but *not* the gift of courage, the greatest virtue.

Nestor wisely suggests that they collect their wits and have a feast to stabilize nerves and fears. Then he carefully lays the plans by which they can entice Achilles back into their service. Nestor's argument is eloquent and Agamemnon consents to give in to Achilles, confess himself in the wrong, and offer a handsome gift to him: seven tripods (bronze three-legged stands), ten talents of gold (we do not know what modern weight corresponds to the bronze-age "talent"), twenty "bright" pots, twelve racing horses, seven women captured on the island of Lesbos, plus the girl he took away from him, Briseis—the act that triggered Achilles' anger in the first place.

COMMENTARY: Note how Agamemnon hopes to minimize his arrogant selfishness by offering to return Briseis as one of many gifts. He will also give Achilles twenty of the most beautiful Trojan women when they have captured Troy, and upon their return to Greece will honor him with one of his daughters in marriage and with the friendship of his son Orestes. He will give him seven walled cities near Pylos.

Then a party of men is selected to go to Achilles and make the offer. Odysseus, the cleverest persuader, is chosen, and the warrior Aias, and Achilles' boyhood teacher, Phoinix. The royal heralds Odios and Eurybates go along also.

Odysseus makes the offer after Achilles has received them with all due honor (offering them food and wine), but Achilles refuses. All of his resentment against Agamemnon spills out in his violent reply. He has been unappreciated, he says; he has been used selfishly by the greedy Agamemnon. He clearly enjoys the plight of the Greeks, for now they realize the value of his battle prowess. The Trojans, he points out, had never ventured beyond the oak tree that stands outside the Skaian Gate when he was in the battles; now they have driven the Greeks to the sea (he does not mention that, through the advocacy of his mother Thetis, he had asked Zeus to make this happen). The proffered gifts are all too little, and Achilles suspects that Agamemnon has changed his mind not out of just reconsideration but because he wants Achilles to save his neck. He arrogantly and triumphantly announces that he will sail away tomorrow morning, abandoning the war altogether.

He reminds them of his fate: to die gloriously while he is young, or to have a peaceful long life without glory. Achilles chooses the latter.

The ambassadors are stunned by the harshness of the refusal. The aged Phoinix, who has known Achilles since he was a child, is most shocked by the open taunt of the threat to sail away while the Greek ships may be burning. In an old man's passionate and tearful plea (to be paralleled in Book XI by old Nestor's plea to Patroklos), Phoinix tells of his own life and how he has always loved Achilles as a son (Phoinix was placed under a curse by the gods and can have no children of his own). "It is not your right to have no pity," he says, "when the very gods can be implored."

Phoinix then tells the history of Meleager (lines 529-599), the Kalydonian hero who alone could save his people but who, through surly anger, would not help them until the last minute. But when he did help them and drove away the enemy, they gave him no honor. It is a tale with a nicely broad moral for Achilles to digest. Achilles replies that he wants no honor from the Greeks, who have insulted him.

Aias next entreats Achilles. He is a blunt, honest soldier, with no gift for speaking. He merely blurts out that he cannot understand Achilles' turning his back on his friends, all those Greeks who have *not* insulted him and beside whom he has fought and played in good fellowship.

Achilles replies that he will not think of fighting again until Hektor has come all the way to the ships. He mentions, archly, that he doesn't think Hektor will come near *his* ships. Aias' unadorned plea at least draws a better answer from Achilles than the other two. The ambassadors return with their bad news, and Diomedes counsels the Greeks to make the best of it and forget Achilles, who, he says, will not fight until the gods move him.

COMMENTARY: The rhythm of the *Iliad* is now becoming an alternation of hope and despair. Zeus, holding his scales of justice, has been keeping the battles an even balance of victory and defeat for both sides. The Trojans know that Hektor is their sole hope, and they (and Hektor) know that his presence in the battles must be meted out sparingly. The Greeks, on the other hand, do not have the presence of their hero at all. The two contentions that underlie the entire poem are now in direct conflict with each other.

In this book we see Patroklos for the first time.

He is Achilles' companion, whose action will trigger the central tragedy of the poem.

Homer's characterization of Achilles here is one of the most brilliant of his two epics. It is brilliant because of its violence and power to shock. It is one of the strongest, clearest pictures of a stubborn, angry man in all literature. Yet it is typically Homeric in that the characterization is of an absolute passion, a flat, irrevocable refusal, even though there are psychological and circumstantial forces—subtly placed before our eyes all along—that will dissolve Achilles' stubbornness.

The design of Book IX is starkly dramatic: it begins in fear and despair, moves to hope, then falls deeper into fear and despair when the hope collapses.

Book X: The Book of the Stalking Spies

At the end of the last book the Greek warriors, fearful and realizing that without Achilles' help they had only their own strength to rely on, went to sleep. This book begins with each of the chiefs, one by one, waking up, too filled with anxiety to sleep.

Agamemnon wakes first, arms himself, and (because of the cold night) puts on his lion skin. Menelaos wakes and puts on his leopard-skin cloak. Agamemnon wakes Nestor and suggests that they check the guards to see that they are awake. Odysseus and Diomedes join them, and, in a whispered council, they plan to send spies to the Trojan camp to see if they can learn anything of their plans.

Odysseus and Diomedes volunteer and set out fully armed. Pallas Athena sends a heron as a sign to signal her pleaure. Meanwhile Hektor, too, has had the same idea and chooses a spy, Dolon, to go into the Greek camp. He wears a wolf's hide.

COMMENTARY: Note how carefully Homer had added the element of stalking and predatory stealthiness by putting his characters in this book into animal pelts. Odysseus wears an especially symbolic helmet, one stolen by his notorious thief of a grandfather, Autolykos (whose name means *Wolf*).

As the two parties traverse the dark no-man's-land between the two camps, Odysseus detects Dolon and goes for him. Dolon bolts. Odysseus throws a spear above him that sticks in the earth before his feet. Dolon freezes in his tracks, his teeth chattering. Odysseus promises him his life, learns from him the positions of the armies in Hektor's camp—and cuts off his head, which was "still speaking" as it fell.

Odysseus and Diomedes sneak into the Thracian camp, drive away the horses and kill many of the men in their sleep. They return triumphantly, with the horses, to the Greek camp, bathe first in the sea, and then in their bathtubs, and have breakfast.

COMMENTARY: This book is all one skillfully told episode of spy work, and is inserted as a last example of the kind of warfare that went on in the first nine years of the war: raids and counter-raids. It is a cool piece of treachery characteristic of Odysseus in the tense moment before the two armies will clash in the greatest encounter of the war (except for the burning of the city itself).

The scene has a developmental unity. At its beginning, Agamemnon can see the watchfires of the Trojans, hear their flutes and their voices. The middle section of the book takes place in darkness—an ominous darkness with corpses underfoot, left on the battlefield from the day's fighting. The end is back in the Greek camp; the anxiety and fear remain, yet a minor triumph has cheered them a little.

Book XI: The Book of The Brothers

This book recounts the battle in which Hektor had hoped to burn the Greek ships but is, instead, pushed back to his city walls.

Dawn and Hate (two very different goddesses) rise together. The dew in the early light is red, like blood. We are shown Agamemnon dressing in his armor—Homer's sign that he is to have his moment of glory, his *aristeia*. It is an elaborate suit of armor, described in detail (lines 15-46)—on his shield is the staring, terrible face of the Gorgon, an emblem to ward off evil (wide eyes, grimacing mouth, jutting tongue, fangs).

Just as he finishes putting on his armor a roll of thunder comes
to show the approval of Athena and Hera. Hektor, in contrast,
is like a flash of lightning in his bronze armor. (The bitter,
angry Agamemnon is like rolling thunder; Hektor, defender of
his people, is all brightness.)

The Greeks and Trojans make a long battle-line and clash.
Homer compares them to two rows of harvesters, with scythes,
and each army is a field of wheat to the other. But the Greeks
soon get the upper hand and Agamemnon goes *berserk* (this
is the right English word for the battle madness; in the Norse
and Saxon armies of Northern Europe the unstoppable warrior
was called a *berserker*). He slays Bienor and then Bienor's
hetairos (close friend and battle companion) Oïleus. Then he
mutilates Peisandros and Hippolochos, sons of Antimachos who,
in the early days of the war, had suggested to the Trojans
that they murder Menelaos and Odysseus when they came to
bargain with the Trojans inside the city. Agamemnon kills Isos
and Antiphos, brothers, and both sons of Priam.

COMMENTARY: Throughout this book we get the killing of
                  brothers or of close friends, a relationship that
for the Greeks was as strong as that of brotherhood. We
shall see why when we look at the total structure of
the book, for it is here that we begin to see the rôle that
Achilles' *hetairos* Patroklos is going to play. This theme
also underlines the brotherly solicitude that we see
among the wounded Greeks. Homer deepens our sense of
pity with these tales of brothers and friends dying together (or coming to each other's rescue) before he
describes the utterly pitiless slaughter that begins in
the next book.

Agamemnon is twice compared to a forest fire roaring
through the Trojan army. The Trojans are pushed back to the
Skaian Gate. Zeus sees that it is time to interfere, but does
not want Hektor to face Agamemnon while the battle madness
is upon him. He sends Iris to tell Hektor that his signal for
going into battle will be the wounding of Agamemnon.

At this point Homer makes another invocation to the
Muse (as at the beginning of the poem), for the *aristeia* of
Agamemnon is to give way to that of Hektor.

Agamemnon is stopped when he fights the brothers Iphi-

damas and Koön. He kills them both, but Koön wounds Agamemnon in the elbow—with a pain compared to that of childbirth. Agamemnon is taken off the battlefield in his chariot.

Diomedes and Odysseus take over the initiative, until
both are put out of the battle. Diomedes is shot in the foot by
Paris. Odysseus is surrounded and fights his way out of the
encirclement, killing man after man. The Trojan Sokos pierces
Odysseus' shield with a spear, and thinks that he has killed
him, only to walk away and be transfixed himself through the
back: Pallas has not let Odysseus be killed.

Aias and Menelaos come to Odysseus' rescus. Aias is
compared to a flooding river among the troops. On the left
flank of the battle-line (where Hektor is raging), the Greek
doctor Makhaon is wounded and old Nestor comes out in his
chariot to rescue him.

Hektor then moves over to the part of the battle where
Aias is causing havoc and (together with Kebriones) puts such
pressure there that Aias retreats, little by little. The wounded
Greek Eurypylos rallies the army around him, and rescues the
trapped Aias. The Trojans again have the offensive, "fighting
like shining fire."

The battle goes on. Our attention, however, is moved to
the Greek camp, where Nestor is shown bringing in the wounded
doctor Makhaon. Achilles, standing on the stern of one of his
beached ships, has been watching the battle. He is curious to
see who it is that Nestor has rescued, and sends Patroklos to
find out. Curiosity (the weakest form of solicitude, but the beginning of it) does what the strong entreaties of his friends
could not! "And here," says Homer, "was the beginning of his
tragedy" (line 603).

Then the scene shifts to Nestor and Makhaon in Nestor's
tent. Hekamede, the old man's concubine and servant, prepares a meal for the exhausted old men, a typically Greek meal
that is still served in Crete and the Greek hinterlands: barley
bread, honey, and a cup of Pramnian wine with goat's cheese
grated into it, and an onion to munch while drinking the wine.

While they are eating, Patroklos arrives. Nestor quietly
sees his opportunity and begins reminiscing about his prowess

as a young man. As he talks (and his tales are obviously whoppers, and have grown in the telling over the years), he slyly keeps bringing up Achilles, hinting what glory he might have if he were all on fire for glory (such as Nestor has won) rather than sulking in his tent. Finally, he openly begs Patroklos to persuade Achilles, or (and here he strikes home) at least go into the fighting himself wearing Achilles' armor, to frighten the Trojans.

Patroklos is filled with pity at the sight of the many Greek wounded. He sees that all the greatest warriors are hurt and out of the fighting. He stops long enough to cut an arrow from Eurypylos' thigh, and dresses the wound.

COMMENTARY: Patroklos' visit is indeed the beginning of Achilles' tragedy, for the way is now opened whereby he will be brought into the fighting, and it is not a way that either he or the chiefs had thought of.

Note how Homer uses the imagery of fire and flood throughout: men in destructive anger imitating the ravishes of nature. Homer is a master of *adumbration* —laying down a trail of hints and forebodings before he announces a theme openly. One of the best examples is the theme of the brothers in this book, leading us to the brotherly friends Achilles and Patroklos, whose *philia* (a Greek word stronger than *friendship* but not quite *love* in our romantic sense of the word) will now change the whole action of the poem.

Book XII: The Book of The Battle of The Greek Wall

At the beginning of this book we have a picture of how, in the future, the gods will destroy the Greek wall—it was built without sacrifices to the gods—and at the end of the book we see Trojans tearing it down with their own hands: Sarpedon pulling it down and Hektor smashing one of its gates with a boulder. So the action is framed between two images of the wall's destruction.

Poseidon and Apollo, the gods famous for their quickness to take vengeance, will eventually destroy the wall; meanwhile the Trojans undertake the task themselves. The Greeks are withdrawing behind it; the gates are kept open but guarded so that last-minute escapes can be made. When the Trojans arrive in their chariots, they discover that the ditch before the wall contains sharpened stakes. This means that they must dismount and storm the wall on foot. The Trojan army is divided into five battalions, to be commanded by Hektor, Paris, Deïphobos, Aeneas, and Sarpedon.

Asios the Trojan is the first to charge, causing a battle at one of the gates. As other Trojans move up, the Greeks throw stones at them that fall as thick as snow.

A sign appears in the sky. An eagle carrying a snake is bitten by its prey and drops it. The snake falls among the Trojans. Poulydamas interprets this as a bad sign for the Trojans, but Hektor, who is impatient with signs, rebukes him, saying that the defense of their country is the only sign the Trojans need—and they can read that in their hearts. Hektor then gives orders for an all-out attack, and Zeus, who is with him, sends a dust storm to blind the Greeks, "to confuse the Achaeans and give mighty deeds to the Trojans and to Hektor."

The two Aiantes stride along the wall, encouraging the Greeks. The Trojans attempt to scale the wall along its length, and the Greeks fight on the top. The Lycians, fighting for the Trojans, are the most successful, and the two Aiantes and Teukros the archer are called to defend the spot. There is fierce fighting. Sarpedon, who is among the Lycians, pulls down part of the wall with his hands, making an entry through which the Lycians pour.

Hektor, meanwhile, has picked up a boulder (which, Homer notes, two men could not pick up in these weaker days) and smashed a gate with it, a gate doubly bolted inside. He enters, and his battalion follows him, causing panic among the Greeks inside.

COMMENTARY: The book ends abruptly here, at the midpoint of the poem. For the Greeks, the very worst has happened. The Trojans, however, are not much better off. Poulydamas, the bird-reader, has pointed out to Hektor that it is an awkward strategy to enter the gates, for the Trojans can easily be trapped inside with their line of retreat cut off. Hektor is counting on Zeus' promise sent by Iris, that he will be given honor once Agamemnon is wounded.

As Hektor smashes the gate, he calls to the Trojans to bring "inhuman fire." The Greeks are at last trapped between fire and water: their darkest fear.

Book XIII: The Book of The Battle Inside The Wall

Once Hektor's forces storm the wall and are fighting inside, Zeus turns his attention to other lands and people: the Tracian horsemen, the knife-fighting Mysians, the Hippomolgoi "who drink milk," and the just and pious Abioi.

COMMENTARY: No profounder example of Olympian indifference occurs in Greek literature than Zeus' loss of interest in the Trojan War at this tense moment. It is characteristic of Homer that he should, at this point, indicate that the world is full of other people, and that they are as important to Zeus as the Greeks and Trojans.

Poseidon, however, watches the battle, and takes pity on the Greeks. In four steps he strides from the island Samos, where he had been watching Troy, to his golden water-palace at Aigai (whereabouts no longer known, if it ever existed). There he dresses in gold, mounts his chariot and, drawn by horses that race on water, comes to Troy, where he hides his team in a cave. Disguised as Kalkhas he goes to Telemonian Aias and the lesser Aias and tells them that they can save the Greeks. So that they can know he is a god, he turns into a hawk before their eyes and flies above them. Poseidon has given them extraordinary strength and the exhilaration of self-confidence.

Poseidon then encourages the rest of the Greeks, especially those who had fallen into despair and were weeping. Battle is evil, he says, but to keep from battle is a worse evil.

Hektor's coming through the wall is compared (lines 135-142) to an avalanche of stones down a forest slope. The fighting is so dense that the horse tails of the helmets flop against each other in the battle-line. The fighting reaches a chaotic pitch. The two Aiantes have the battle madness. At one terrible moment Aias Oileïdes cuts off a Trojan head and throws it so that it lands at Hektor's feet.

Poseidon then inspires Idomeneus, leader of the Cretan forces, who takes Meriones with him to the left flank. Poseidon

moves among the troops, inciting, but cannot openly fight, for
fear of incurring the wrath of his elder brother Zeus. Homer explains here that Zeus' will is really deviously for the Greeks, in
that he is fulfilling Thetis's prayer that Achilles be given honor
by having the Greeks humiliated. Nevertheless, for the moment Poseidon and Zeus are at cross purposes, and the fighting
is the bitterer for it.

Idomeneus kills Othryoneus, who was betrothed to Priam's
daughter Kassandra and who had offered instead of the usual
bride-price to drive the Greeks from Troy—giving Idomeneus
the material for a cruel insult as he kills Othryoneus.

Idomeneus' *aristeia* rages on, and the descriptions of the
carnage become more terrible. Deiphobos, having killed Hypse-
nor to avenge Asios, boasts that Asios goes to Hades' house
with a glad heart, seeing that his murderer is just behind him.
Idomeneus kills Alkathoös, Ankhises' son-in-law, in an eerie and
curious scene. Poseidon bewitches Alkathoös so that he cannot
move and must stand as motionless as a tree while Idomeneus
forces his spear into his heart. He falls, "but his heart was still
beating and made the spear rise and fall."

There is a tangled battle between Aeneas and Idomeneus,
but their guards do most of the fighting. Homer reports every
spear thrust with graphic care. Menelaos strikes out both of
Peisandros' eyes. Over the corpse, while he is stripping it of
armor, Menelaos makes an angry speech against the Trojans—
it is he they have most wronged, having stolen his wife Helen.
The close of the speech is an epitomé of the Greek frustration
with the Trojans, and its imagery is perfectly apt in the midst
of this orgy of brutal death. The speech is hurled at Zeus, and
questions his wisdom:

> . . . these Trojans,
> Who can't get too full of deadly battle at close-quarters,
> Though in everything there is satiety: in sleep and in love,
> In sweet song and in blameless dance,
> A man is more eager to get his fill of these things than
> Of war. But the Trojans are gluttons for battle. *(633-639)*

The battle continues. The book thus far has been describing the left flank of the wall, where the Trojans are being
bested. Hektor is fighting at the other end, and there the Greeks
are getting the worst of it. Poulydamas takes Hektor aside

and counsels him before there is total confusion and the Trojan forces are so scattered among the Greeks that they will be overwhelmed at any moment. The two Aiantes are moving through the left flank like a yoke of oxen. Poulydamas cautions Hektor to rally the troops to make a unified fighting force, reminding him that Achilles may unexpectedly join the battle. Hektor goes one way, Poulydamas another, and between them they marshal the Trojan forces. Hektor has occasion to scold Paris, whom he meets. As he is taking new command, Hektor meets Aias, who taunts him. Hektor calls him an ox. The battle reengages.

COMMENTARY: This book is solid battle, and is, in a sense, one of the most static books of the epic. It has the design of a net: every point is connected to every other. The episodes are entirely of duels and woundings and death, all vividly given until we are numbed by the hideousness of the details. But in another sense it is one of the most realistic of the books, for a battle at close quarters must be just such a confusing tangle. Homer keeps his sense of proportion: the dead are identified with enough information to prevent their being mere names, and he has worked in those details that elicit pity. All this carnage comes dangerously close to ruining its own effect by taking on the semblance of a slaughter house, where we are aware of helplessness and pain but not especially of tragedy. It is Homer's triumph that he can keep a tragic sense while satiating us with horrendous and ugly slaughters.

The theme of the book that appears everywhere is that of gluttony, for the impact of such mass killing on the senses is overpowering. At the end of the book Hektor threatens Aias, the largest of the Greeks, and says that he will glut dogs and birds with his corpse. Menelaos' sickened cry to Zeus is built around the imagery of gluttony. To enforce this theme with stark obviousness, there is much imagery of spilled bowels, wounds in the stomach, throat, and buttocks—all done with calculated artistic impact. War is heroic to Homer, but it is also bestial and brutish.

The book began with an ironic note, pointing out that all this slaughter was happening on one little

spot of earth, and noting that life went on in the rest of
the broad world. So at the end, the screams and shouts
of the warriors go up into the empty air ("the glittering
cold air of Zeus") where, from a perspective that includes all creation, they are utterly insignificant.

As if weighed and meted out on Zeus' just
scales, neither side gets any advantage in the course of
the action.

Book XIV: The Book of Zeus and Hera

In this book the Greeks seize the offensive again, with
Poseidon's help.

The book begins with the scene that ended Book XII:
the meal of Nestor and the wounded Makhaon in Nestor's tent.
Nestor hears the tumult of the battle and comes out to see, to
his horror, that the Trojans have broken through the wall. He
quickly decides against going into the battle and joins a council of the chiefs, most of whom are wounded and out of the
fighting. He finds them looking on helplessly. Agamemnon is
in despair, and again suggests that they flee in the ships.
Odysseus rebukes him, not only for cowardice but for not seeing
that a preparation for fleeing in the night would demoralize
the fighters in the battle now. Diomedes says that they must
themselves go back to the fighting, wounded or not.

At this point Poseidon, disguised as an old man, comes
to them and tells Agamemnon that the moment is coming when
the Trojans will retreat across the plain. Then he disappears
and yells like nine thousand men (to show that he is a god).
The cry galvanizes both the leaders and the men in the battle,
and the Greeks are refreshed and renewed in courage.

The scene now shifts to Olympos, where Hera is pleased
by Poesidon's encouragement. She looks to Ida, where Zeus
sits, and her heart is filled with hate. But she has a happy
thought: she will seduce Zeus, and put him to sleep afterwards,
so that Poseidon can continue to help the Greeks.

Her preparation is at once wonderfully comic and deeply
sensuous. She locks herself in her golden bedroom, bathes in
ambrosia, smears herself with olive oil (one could smell her
fragrance on earth, Homer says, and throughout heaven),
combs her hair, puts on an embroidered dress ("with many

pictures on it"), a golden brooch, a belt with a hundred tassels hanging from it, earrings with jewels shaped like mulberries, and wraps a turban around her head, leaving the ends to hang down by her cheeks.

She then begs Aphrodite for a charm, telling her that she is going to patch up the loveless marriage of Grandfather Oceanos and Grandmother Tethys. Aphrodite takes from around her breasts her magic breastband on which all the acts of love are embroidered. This Hera tucks into her bosom and leaps in one bound from Olympos to Lemnos, the home of the god Hypnos, Sleep. She offers him a golden chair with a footstool if he will come with her and put Zeus into a deep sleep after she has seduced him. He refuses, knowing the punishment for acting against the father of gods and men. She then offers him the nymph Pasithea, one of the Graces, and he accepts. They proceed to Ida, where Hypnos takes the form of the kymindis bird while Hera accomplishes her business.

Zeus is immediately stricken with desire for Hera, but she craftily says that she is on the way to Oceanos and Tethys. Zeus is not to be put off. He tells her that he feels more desire for her than he ever felt for Ixion's wife, Danae, Europa, Semele, Alkmena, Demeter, or Leto, or even for Hera herself. He causes a bed of clover, crocus, and hyacinth to spring up, so thick that they can make love on it, and puts a wall of cloud around them.

Once Zeus is asleep, Hypnos goes to Troy and tells Poseidon that he may openly enter the battle for a little while.

The Greeks fight with great fury. Aias fells Hektor with a rock, hitting him in the neck. The Greeks almost capture Hektor, but the Trojans rescue him and take him to the river Skamandros, where he regains consciousness and vomits blood. Aias then kills Satnios (whose mother was a naiad, or water spirit) and Archelochos. Peneleos kills Ilioneus (a grisly scene, in which Ilioneus' eyeball sticks to the point of Peneleus' spear, and is held aloft to the horror of the Trojans). Aias has another *aristeia*, and kills more than any other. The book ends with slaughter.

COMMENTARY: This is a short book, three hundred lines shorter than the previous and two hundred shorter than the next. Its symmetry is obvious: it opens with the battle, shows the seduction of Zeus by Hera, and closes with the battle. Again the immortal happiness of the gods is put in blunt contrast to the misery of mankind.

Hera's seduction of Zeus is an astounding piece of imagery, all flowers and jewels and opulent clothing. The bloody bandages of the wounded are implicitly contrasted to Aphrodite's erotic breastband, the slaughter of men in utmost cruelty to the divine bed of flowers on which Zeus and Hera make love. There is no sharper contrast in the poem than this alignment of human hatred and divine love. Yet Hera is committing a breach of trust (to human eyes) with her lord and husband-brother, while the human beings are fighting in trust and sincerity.

Book XV: The Book of Aias on The Ships

The Trojans are driven across the wall out of the Greek camp; they rally, however, and make a stand by their chariots.

Zeus wakes from his sleep, and looks toward Troy where he sees Hektor out of the battle, dazed and vomiting blood. He also sees his brother Poseidon helping the Greeks. He realizes instantly what has happened and is furious. He reminds Hera of the time he hung her by her wrists and tied anvils to her feet, and threatened any of the gods who might try to come to her aid. Hera replies (with some portion of truth) that she had nothing to do with Poseidon's entering the battle. Zeus sends her to Olympos, to signal Iris and Apollo. But before she goes he discloses to her his plan: Hektor is to kill Achilles' companion, Patroklos, as soon as the Trojans have humiliated the Greeks by burning a ship (his promise to Thetis will then be fulfilled), and Achilles is to kill Hektor. Then, with the help of Athena, Troy will fall.

Hera goes back to Olympos with the speed of thought. The goddess Themis greets her (Themis is of the older generation of gods, the mother of Prometheus). Hera, with characteristic mischief, does not immediately give Zeus' messages but attempts to stir up the wrath of Ares by telling him that his son Askalaphos has been killed in the war. Ares arms, bent on vengeance, but the wise Pallas Athena takes off his armor and forces him to refrain from intervening.

Hera delivers her messages. Apollo and Iris go to Ida, to

take their orders from Zeus. He sends Iris to command Poseidon to leave the battle. Poseidon at first refuses, rehearsing the order of the gods as fate chose them by lot: the three divine brothers were assigned their domains; Zeus got the clouds and air; Hades, the underworld, domain of the dead; and Poseidon got the sea. Olympos and the earth, however, belong to all three. He therefore sees no law or reason why he should obey his brother. Iris reminds him of the Furies, executors of the divine vengeance, and that they always side with the elder in a quarrel. Poseidon relents.

Zeus sends Apollo to put strength into Hektor. He comes as "a hawk, murderer of the dove" (images of war and peace, then as now). Apollo discloses himself to the wounded Hektor:

> Have courage now: I am an ally sent from Ida
> By Kronos' son, to be with you and protect you,
> Phoibos Apollo of the golden sword, who has before now
> Defended you and the high citadel of your people. (254-257)

Hektor and Apollo go back to the battle together. The sight of Hektor frightens the Greeks, for a man whom Aias has hit with a rock cannot usually recuperate so soon. They cannot see Apollo, who is invisible and who carries before him the divine *aegis*—the magic goatskin against the power of which nothing can stand.

The Trojans storm the Greek wall again, urged on by the tremendous battle cry of Apollo. Apollo kicks down the wall as the sea destroys a sand castle made by a child. The Greeks panic in their hearts but hold fast in a fury of fighting.

Nestor prays to Zeus, who answers his prayer with a roll of thunder. The Greeks are so hard-pressed that they begin fighting from the beached ships, using the long grappling hooks that are normally used for sea-fighting.

As the new battle rages, Homer shifts back to the scene at the end of Book XII, where Patroklos was helping the wounded Greeks and pondering how he might bring Achilles into the battle. He decides to try personal persuasion. (Homer is careful to show what a slow process the conversion of Achilles is, how a suggestion of Nestor and the plea of Aias must grow slowly in Patroklos' mind.)

Hektor tries without success to set fire to the ships. Aias and his brother Teukros move from ship to ship, beating back the Trojans. There is a personal feud now between Hektor and Aias, though they do not get a chance to come together. Each forms a nucleus, however, around which each army is organized. Teukros, about to shoot Hektor with an arrow, has his bow broken by Zeus.

Aias shouts a speech of encouragement to the Greeks. Like all speeches of the honest, blunt Aias, it is direct and forceful. He asks the Greeks if they think they can walk back to Greece over the ocean. Hektor, he says, has not come to invite them to a dance. This is the decisive hour, the one great time to have the battle madness. Hektor, he reminds them, is a man defending his country, his wife, and his child. If he dies he is still accomplishing his task.

The Greeks encircle each ship "with a fence of their own bodies clad in bronze." Hektor's battle rage grows to a fierceness: he foams at the mouth, his eyes glitter, and the cheekguards of his helmet bounce up and down as he screams for fire and drives his troops against the Greeks.

Zeus sits calmly on Mount Ida, waiting for so much as a single ship to blaze up, for then he will have carried out his promise to Thetis, and can proceed to crush Troy.

As the Trojans push in like hungry mountain lions into a herd of cattle, Nestor cries to the Greeks that he implores them at their knees (the Greek mode of supplication) to remember their homeland and their wives, and to fight for them. "He spoke these things, and roused their hearts and their fighting spirit."

Aias striding from ship to ship is compared to a bareback rider with four horses, who can switch from horse to horse as they gallop. In his fury, Hektor reaches a ship and climbs the prow, hanging onto it and screaming for fire to be brought. But each time fire is brought, the Greeks kill the bearer, and the book ends in the furor of battle, the Greeks defending their ships from the decks, the Trojans coming on persistently with the help of Apollo.

COMMENTARY: This tumultuous book with its desperate and angry fighting foreshadows the end of the epic, and represents the midpoint of the action. What follows is the resolution of the action that has gone before. The Greeks have reached the limit of their resources; all the strength they have left is symbolized by the noble Aias, who has been compared throughout to a wall. He is the personification of force raw and simple. Every Greek setback has reduced the Greek fighting power to the common denominator of the basic infantryman. Aias is heroic (witness his noble, honest speech in this book) but he is limited to the skills of which he is the master: oxlike force. All the Greeks who represent the other kind of soldier—the clever strategist, the swift and lithe warrior —are wounded, except of course Achilles.

Aias is a shield; Achilles a javelin. Aias is a city wall; Achilles, an eagle with iron talons and beak. Hektor combines in one person the strength of Aias and the striking skill of Achilles.

Note how Homer, in these central battle books, uses the rhythm of advance and retreat, of hope and despair, of victory and defeat. The war is still a contest (Homer has twice evoked the image of a tug-of-war); in the next book it will grow into a tragedy, as Zeus predicts to Hera in the beginning of the book.

Book XVI: The Book of Patroklos' Death

Patroklos, his heart moved with pity for the plight of the dying and trapped Greeks, comes to Achilles, as this book opens, weeping "like a spring of dark water"—the same image used of Agamemnon's tears of despair in Book IX.

Achilles (who knows full well why Patroklos is crying) asks him why he weeps like a girl wanting to be picked up by her mother. Are not their fathers, Menoitios and Peleus, still alive? These are an angry man's taunts. And his last jibe is to ask if he could be crying for the Greeks, whose arrogance has brought misfortune on their heads?

Patroklos answers in good faith, telling Achilles that the

leaders are all wounded. "You have no pity," he says. "Peleus the horse-rider was not your father, nor Thetis your mother. You are the child of a rock and the cold sea." (Lines 33-35.)

He then asks that if there is some reason, unknown to him, some prophecy of the gods perhaps, why Achilles cannot go into the fighting. If so, then at least he should allow Patroklos to come to the aid of the Greeks, wearing Achilles' armor.

Achilles' heart is softened. He says that he never intended to be angry forever; and consents to Patroklos' request. Patroklos, it is agreed between them, is to drive the Trojans from the ships and keep them from setting fire to the navy. He is not to pursue them across the plain. Achilles will do that when the time comes.

While they are talking, the Greeks are weakening in their defense. Hektor whacks off the end of Aias' spear with his sword, thus giving the Trojans the opportunity to set fire to the ship Aias is defending.

Achilles sees this, slaps both his thighs with his hands, and hastily arms Patroklos and the rest of his army—the Myrmidons, "ant men," who number 2,500 soldiers. Like the Trojans, they are divided into five battalions, commanded by Menesthios, Eudoros, Peisandros, Phoinix, and Alkimedon. Patroklos is dressed in Achilles' magnificent armor (and the charioteer Automedon hitches to the chariot Achilles' two immortal horses, Xanthos (Yellow) and Balios (Dapple) and a third, ordinary horse named Pedasos (Pounder).

Achilles takes from his locker a golden drinking cup used only for sacrifices and pours wine to Zeus and prays that the god give Patroklos glory and a safe return. Zeus grants the former, denies the latter, for Patroklos will not return alive.

The Myrmidons move out of camp like hornets from a nest. They race to the Greek ships and fall on the Trojans who, at first sight, imagine that Patroklos is Achilles.

There is a strong battle in which the Trojans are beaten from the ships (where the Greeks have put out the fires). Patroklos has his *aristeia*, killing many, but his big moment (before he meets Hektor) is to kill Sarpedon, the Trojan hero who first made a gap in the Greek wall. They engage "like

crooked beaked vultures with hooks for claws, screaming shrilly."
Zeus wants to save Sarpedon, but Hera won't let him, for fear
that all the other gods with favorites will break Zeus' rule and
come and confuse the fighting. Sarpedon is a mortal son of
Zeus, and Zeus weeps to see him die.

In the duel the first two spear throws go awry: Patroklos
kills Sarpedon's *summakhos* (literally co-fighter, or sergeant),
and Sarpedon kills the horse Pedasos. In the next cast Sarpedon
misses, and is killed by a direct hit to the heart. He falls roaring,
clutching at the bloody dust. As he dies he asks his companion,
Glaukos, to defend his body and to avenge his death. But
Glaukos is wounded and cannot fight. He prays to Apollo who
heals his wound, and sends him to rally the Trojans around
Sarpedon's body. Hektor himself comes raging, and a great
battle centers on Sarpedon, with many deaths. Homer compares the sound of the fighting to lumberjacks felling a forest.

Zeus (who ponders whether this is the right moment to
give Patroklos his death, and thus precipitate the entry of
Achilles) sends Apollo down to bring the body of Sarpedon
to his native Lycia, where it can be buried by his kinsmen. But
before Apollo can get there, Patroklos has stripped it of armor,
which he sends back as a prize to the Greek camp.

So great is Patroklos' might that he could have pushed
on (disobeying Achilles) and stormed Troy, except that Apollo
stops him. Three times he tries to run up the sloping wall.
Apollo tells him that it is not for him, or even for Achilles, to
take Troy. Apollo then sends Hektor to stop Patroklos forever.

The duel in which Patroklos dies is a confused one. It begins with Hektor (inconclusively) in a wrestling match from
which they are disengaged by the fury of the fighting around
them. Apollo strikes Patroklos with the flat of his hand, stunning
him. Then Euphorbos stabs him between the shoulders with a
spear. Hektor, however, administers the death blow—a sword
thrust through the abdomen.

Dying, Patroklos tells Hektor that he will be killed by
Achilles. Hektor asks him if it is not just as likely that Achilles
be killed by him. But dead men do not reply to rhetorical
questions.

COMMENTARY: Everyone who speaks of Patroklos calls him "kind, gentle, tender." He was raised with the slightly younger Achilles, and the two were fast friends from early childhood. He is a man under a peculiar fate, with a tragic warp to his existence, who, as Homer says, "innocently asks for his own death." He was an exile from his native Opous in his boyhood, after he accidentally killed a playmate in a quarrel over a game. His father Menoitios asked Peleus, Achilles' father, to adopt him (for murderers were ostracized, as Homer explains in several other examples in the two epics). As if to atone for his quick temper, he became a man of selfless devotion, a man of solicitude. Rachel Bespaloff says in her study of the *Iliad* (see BIBLIOGRAPHY) that Patroklos is a kind of mirror in which the selfish, violent Achilles can imagine he sees himself in a purer form. Among the Greeks Patroklos stands out as a charmingly innocent, compassionate man, lacking the lion-like rapacity of warriors like Diomedes and Achilles. Yet violence is in him: we see that clearly when he goes into battle. He is worthy of Achilles' armor. There is a kinship between Hektor and Patroklos in that they are both kind and generous men. Part of the tragedy of war is that such men must kill each other.

The design of this book is self-contained. It is like a tragedy of the kind Greek authors will write three centuries later in Athens. Patroklos, out of compassion for the weakening Greek army, releases the violence that saves the Greeks but destroys him in its course. It also releases the forces that will destroy Hektor and even Achilles: the prophecy that the dying Patroklos makes of Hektor's death is paralleled later by the prophecy of Achilles' death spoken by the dying Hektor. This is the pivotal book of the epic, the center of all its action. Zeus' promise to Thetis is fulfilled, for the Trojans have set fire to a few ships, and the full measure of humiliation that Achilles wanted has been exacted. The contention between Agamemnon and Achilles is now over, for it dissolves in the more urgent anger of Achilles at Hektor.

We should also note how Homer diminishes the glory that Hektor might have for the death of Patroklos by having three forces cause the murder; Hektor only gives the finishing blow.

Book XVII: The Book of the Fight for Patroklos' Body

As a cow stands protectively over her first-born calf while it is too weak to stand—so runs Homer's graphic simile—Menelaos stands over Patroklos. Euphorbos, one of the killers of Patroklos, challenges Menelaos, not only because he wants to despoil the man he has just brought down but because he has a personal feud with Menelaos, the slayer of Euphorbos' brother. But Melenaos kills him instead. His death is described with a special pity and care (in contrast to the antomical horror of the descriptions in the preceding book):

> Right through the soft part of the neck went the spearhead,
> He fell with a heavy thud and his armor clanged;
> His hair, beautiful as the Graces, was soaked with blood,
> Those tresses caught up with gold and silver to form the
>   shape of a wasp.
> As a young shoot of a vigorous olive tree, raised by a man
> In a lonely place, where plenty of water wets it so that
> It blooms well, and gusts of wind from all directions
> Shake it, and it blossoms with white flowers,
> But then a wind comes suddenly in a mighty storm, twists it
> Out of the earth, and stretches it flat on the ground,
> Thus was Euphorbos of the ashen spear, Panthoös' son,
> When Menelaos, son of Atreus, killed him. . . .

Apollo is determined that Hektor shall have Patroklos' armor and urges him to avenge Euphorbos. Hektor's face "looks like raging fire" and with a great battle scream he drives Menelaos from the body and strips it of its armor. But before he can cut off the head to put on a spike, Menelaos brings Aias, who drives Hektor from the body. Aias stands over the body like a lion over its cub.

Meanwhile, there is a fight for the body of the Trojan Sarpedon, which Glaukos urges Hektor to defend. Hektor puts on the armor of Achilles that he has stripped from Patroklos. This is an important moment, for by this act, as Zeus notes with sadness on Olympos, Hektor assures his own death. It is the sign that he takes full responsibility for Patroklos' death.

Patroklos' body now becomes the center of a battle, with each side alternately driving the other away. Corpses pile on top of and around Patroklos. Hektor and Aeneas are the major contenders among the Trojans; Menelaos and Aias among the Greeks. Many individual duels are described.

Just outside the struggle, the immortal horses that brought Patroklos into the battle stand and weep.

Zeus is to give the Trojans the victory until sundown. The paralyzing shock of the appearance of the Myrmidons has been neutralized by the death of Patroklos and the god-given resistance of the Trojans. Aias, the blunt-tongued, cries out against Zeus' "shameless" patronage of Troy. Hektor and Aeneas attempt to steal the horses that stand and weep for Patroklos, but Automedon, the charioteer saves them with Zeus' help.

So furious and thick is the fighting that no one has told Achilles of Patroklos' death, and Menelaos remembers that this terrible news has to be told. The Greeks feel that Achilles will most certainly enter the fighting, and they wonder what he will do for armor.

Aias and Menelaos finally, with an escort of warriors, manage to carry Patroklos' body from the torrential battle "and the endless thunder of horses, chariots, and spear-throwers was always around them." The Greeks call a general retreat, for Hektor and Aeneas tear at them like a hawk among sparrows. The book closes with an image of the broken weapons that litter the plain and the fighting that still goes on "like uncontrollable fire."

COMMENTARY: The defense of a dead warrior's body, to keep it from being stripped of its armor and to save it for a proper funeral, has been an action described repeatedly since the beginning of the poem (Sarpedon's body, for example, in the preceding book). The Greeks and Trojans alike invariably added to defeat the insult of desecration. The ancients believed that until a body had a funeral with the proper rites a soul could not rest in the underworld of Hades but wandered as a miserable ghost.

The determined defense of Patroklos' body is not only because Patroklos was liked and admired and "knew how to be kind to all men" (as Menelaos says) but because he is precious to what the Greeks know is the last resource in which they can hope, Achilles.

The design of the book, like most of the books

of battle fury, follows the rhythms of defense and offense, of rallying and dispersal.

Book XVIII: The Book of Achilles' Shield

The book opens with Nestor's son, the young Antilochos, bringing Achilles the news of Patroklos' death. Achilles knows from his demeanor what has happened, and guesses before he needs to be told. He pours ashes and dust over his head and collapses in grief. Antilochos holds his hands, for fear that he will stab him in anger, and deep in the sea, Achilles' mother, the sea nymph Thetis, weeps and all her handmaidens weep with her.

COMMENTARY: This is one of Homer's most beautifully evocative and mystical passages, for he suspends the flow of the narrative to give the names of the weeping sea nymphs in ten lines of strange, poetic names. It is as if the grief of Achilles is a subject that can be stated but not immediately pursued, and he holds our attention with the repercussions of it in the remote, silver-lined caves of the sea. Homer, like Shakespeare (who named the fairies in *A Midsummer Night's Dream* Puck, Pease-Blossom, Cobweb, Moth, and Mustard Seed), delights to use words as incantations, as here with the names of the nymphs, thirty-three of them in a glittering and breathless list. The names are lovely in themselves as sounds (Kallianassa, Amatheia, Aktaia) but they are also charming for what they mean: Seafoam, Fairbreeze, Blossom, Fleetfoot, Flasher.

In her grief Thetis says that Achilles "sprang up like a young tree, and I cared for him; he was like the finest tree in the grove," and we remember the tree simile that Homer used in the previous book to describe the death of Euphorbos. Though she is mourning for Patroklos, it is Achilles whom she speaks of as if *he* had died. (Throughout the *Iliad* the battles are frequently compared to the felling of forest, or to forest fires—trees are the only things in nature that take as long as man to mature.)

Thetis then rises from the sea to comfort Achilles. She warns him that his own death is near, for it is fated that he is to die soon after Patroklos. (He will die at the Trojan gates, shot by Paris, but this action happens after the time covered by the *Iliad.*) Achilles says that he cares nothing for his own death; that he lives solely to kill Hektor. His anger is "like a bitter smoke in the heart," and yet—because he can do something about it—it is "as sweet as drops of honey."

Thetis promises him that she will have Hephaistos himself, god of fire and smith of the gods, make him a suit of armor, and will bring it to him the next morning.

Meanwhile the Greeks are fighting their way back to the ships with the body of Patroklos. Iris comes from the gods to send Achilles into battle. He cannot go, for he has no armor, and the only armor that will fit his enormous physique is that of Aias, who is in the thick of the fighting. So Achilles goes to the wall, "blazing like fire," and gives a shout so loud that the Trojan horses wheel around in retreat. The shock of this great cry gives the Greeks time enough to pull Patroklos' body from the battlefield. Achilles runs out to walk beside the litter on which Patroklos had been laid.

Night falls on earth, and the Trojans withdraw to the city. There is a council in which Poulydamas argues that they ought to remain inside tomorrow, for Achilles cannot get in. Hektor refuses to be besieged by a single man, and wants to go out and fight him. The Trojans agree with Hektor.

The Greeks mourn all night for Patroklos. Achilles embraces the slashed body and mourns "like a lion, great bearded, whose cubs the hunter stole." He vows not to bury Patroklos until he has brought Hektor's head to the funeral, and twelve young men of the Trojans to be killed on the funeral pyre.

The same night on Olympos, Hephaistos makes the suit of armor that Thetis has asked for. At the time of Hephaistos' expulsion from Olympos (alluded to at the end of the first book), he spent nine years in hiding and Thetis protected him then in her cave in the sea, so he is glad to have the opportunity to do her a favor. He makes a suit of armor the like of which has never been seen before. The armor itself is elaborate (and invincible), but the great shield with its pictures worked into the metal is the important part.

In a hundred and forty lines of description, the remainder

of this book, Homer tells us the design of the shield's face. In circles one within the other, from the boss in the center to the outer rim, there are engraved pictures. They depict the earth, the sea, and the sky, with sun, moon, and the constellations. Then two cities are shown. In one is a marriage procession. In the other there is a quarrel between two men in the market-place, complete with a crowd of people listening and taking part. Then there are pictures of two armies fighting, with Ares and Pallas Athena taking part, and an ambush of shepherds by soldiers, and a battle by the river banks. Then there is a scene of a king's lands, with harvesters, a head of cattle and nine dogs, and a meadow with sheep.

COMMENTARY: We should imagine these scenes in the style of the late eighth century B.C. (as best we can tell from what has survived)—an art that delighted in intricacy, in depicting many things happening at once. The figures would have been schematic rather than realistic, without perspective, yet strongly graphic and clear.

Achilles' shield, brought into the poem at this point, is a symbol of order, of *kosmos* as the Greeks would have said: a word meaning both order and beauty. Homer mentions first the order of the world, the stars and their courses that are beyond the power of Zeus or any known gods. The other end of the scale is man's order, the harvest and the cattle. It is this last order that is being destroyed in the war (as the shield itself shows, and is itself an implement in its destruction). Yet the war grew out of another disorder: Troy's disruption of the rite of marriage which is the first thing shown after the constellations. Only a god could have made so serene a model of the world; the world is many things at once, both war and peace, tranquillity and confusion, love and hate. The shield is an apt symbol for Achilles to bear, for he is now out of the ordinary life of men. Marriages and harvests will go on, but not for Achilles. His own death is near, and he is dedicated to the death of one man and the mourning of another. He has become, as we shall see, an almost abstract design of pure fate, to flash like a meteor, and then go out.

Most of the interaction of gods and men in the poem is from Olympos downward. Twice the action has moved upward, each time for Achilles, both through the intercession of Thetis.

Book XIX: The Book of Achilles Going into Battle

At dawn Thetis brings the armor. Achilles is still embracing Patroklos, and his men are around him. Thetis puts the armor beside him. The men are afraid of it, so divine is it, and turn away, terrified to look at something fresh from the terrible hands of the gods. Achilles looks at it, dreaming of the death of Hektor; his eyes burned under their lids, "like the fire of the sun."

Thetis promises to keep the body of Patroklos from putrefaction, and puts ambrosia through the nostrils and heals the wounds with "red nectar."

Achilles strides up and down the beach, calling the Greeks to assembly. Even the cooks and quartermaster people come, for whom the fighting is usually of no concern. In the assembly Achilles announces that he is ready to fight. He is sorry that the quarrel with Agamemnon happened, and wishes that Briseis had been killed by Artemis before she was captured. "Now," he says, "I put an end to my anger." Agamemnon counters this speech with an apology of his own, an apology which is more of a rationalization of his stupidity and greed than a real apology. His ungenerous mind shows all too clearly as he tries to blame his actions on the goddess Delusion, going into a long explanation (that must have bored everyone present) as to how Delusion had taken in even Zeus. He tells the myth of the birth of Herakles and Eurystheus, wherein Zeus, proud of the child Herakles that was to be born to Alkemene, whom he had seduced, proclaimed that the child to be born that day would be preeminent among men. Whereupon Hera craftily went as a midwife and delivered, prematurely, Eurytheus, before Alkmene could give birth to Herakles.

Two plans are put forward: one, Achilles' is to move into battle without further ado; the other, Odysseus' is to have a feast and formal presentation of the gifts that Agamemnon has offered Achilles. One should not, he explains, fight on an empty stomach. Agamemnon is for Odysseus' plan, and there is a sacrifice (a boar has its throat cut and is thrown into the sea) while Agamemnon swears that he is returning Briseis untouched.

Briseis goes to the bier of Patroklos and weeps, making a funeral speech. Patroklos had been her protector and, in a sense, her sponsor. The other captive women of Achilles and Patroklos weep also, "outwardly for Patroklos, but inwardly for themselves."

Achilles refuses to eat or drink before the battle. This is not only because his purpose is single-minded and he has no patience with any action except the death of Hektor, but also because his food was prepared for him by Patroklos, and the memory of that is too painful for him. Athena secretly puts ambrosia in Achilles' heart, so that he will have strength.

The Greeks move out to battle, thick as snowflakes, their bronze armor flashing to the sky, and the earth trembling under their marching and horses. Achilles puts on the divine armor and mounts his chariot. As he rides out onto the plain, he says to his immortal horses Xanthos and Balios, "Be certain to bring me back as well. Do not leave me there after the fighting, as you left Patroklos."

It is one of the wonderful surprises of the poem that the horses answer! Hera gives Xanthos a voice. He says:

We shall see you safely back this time, strong Achilles.
But the time of your perishing is near, not from us,
But from a great god and the force of destiny. *(408-410)*

Achilles is disturbed by such a strange portent, but he shouts back with spirit that he knows he is to die in Troy, but nevertheless he thinks the Trojans will see all they want to of his fighting before he dies.

COMMENTARY: The action of the book is framed in the supernatural: the armor brought by Thetis at the beginning, the gift of speech in the horse Xanthos at the end. Achilles through the course of the book slowly, steadily rises from prostrate grief to the exhilaration of anger, a process that begins when the divine armor takes his attention from Patroklos to Hektor, and his eyes glow like hot coals.

Note how the emphasis of the plot slides from the forces under Agamemnon to the Myrmidons under

Achilles. The ceremonial return of Briseis—the starting point of the poem—which has been so hotly awaited, happens anticlimactically, and Achilles pays no attention whatever to her or to the gifts. The contention with Agamemnon has evaporated. Nothing matters now except that the utmost price be exacted from the Trojans for the death of Patroklos.

Book XX: The Book of Achilles in Battle

The armies approach each other. On Olympos Zeus has had a complete change of heart. Now that Thetis' promise is fulfilled, he invites the gods to go down and fight as they will among the human armies. Hera, Poseidon, Athena, Hermes, and Hephaistos go to help the Greeks. Ares, Apollo, Artemis, Aphrodite, Leto, and Xanthos, called Skamandros among men (he is the god of the river that runs by Troy) go to the Trojans.

The Trojans go weak in the knees when they see Achilles approaching. It is not Hektor but Aeneas who challenges Achilles. Before their duel, there is a long ritual boasting, such as we have seen several times before. Aeneas tells his family history, emphasizing the fact that his mother is the goddess Aphrodite, while Achilles' is the goddess Thetis. Aeneas' recital is very long (and wonderfully interesting, containing such wonders as horses, bred on mortal mares by the West Wind, that can run along the tassels of a wheatfield) but is scarcely something that Achilles could listen to with patience. Not until Aeneas is saved from his spear does Achilles realize that it wasn't all a pack of boastful lies; Poseidon lifts Aeneas away from the duel. (Aeneas must be saved to lead away a remnant of the Trojans after the destruction of the city.)

Achilles then begins to rage and kill. Hektor wants to face him, but Apollo stays him, saying that he must wait.

Achilles is "like fire, and his heart like red-hot iron." Hektor does manage to meet him, in spite of Apollo, and casts a spear at Achilles, which Pallas Athena blows away with a puff of her breath. Before Achilles can exchange a spear thrust, Apollo hides Hektor in a mist.

Achilles rages "like fire through the dry woods of mountains, with a swift wind to whip it along," and scatters and destroys the Trojans like "an ox trampling over the barley on a threshing floor." The axle of his chariot is red with blood, and the wheels and his hands are bloody.

COMMENTARY: This book begins swiftly and looks as if it is going to move at a fast pace. Homer rarely moves directly in the direction we anticipate, however, and the pace of the book becomes slow in its middle part, with Aeneas' long myth telling, and the abortive attempts of Hektor and Achilles to engage in a duel. Then, all of a sudden, Achilles runs berserk, slaughtering on all sides. This is one of the two great *androktasias* (slaughterings) that he is to have in the *Iliad*. This one is on the plain; the other (in the next book) will be in the river and the river-meadow. Therefore this book and the next form a single unit.

Book XXI: The Book of The Gods in Battle

The Trojan army breaks into halves before Achilles; one half flees across the plain to the city, and Hera shrouds them in mist to keep them out of the action for the moment. The other half flees to the river Skamandros (who, in this book, because he is both a god and a river, is known by his Olympian name of Xanthos), where Achilles drives them into the water. He leaps in after them and kills and kills, until he is weary with slaughter and the river runs red and is all but dammed with bodies. He choose twelve of the living, binding them with leather thongs, to be the human sacrifice at Patroklos' funeral.

As he comes out of the water, he sees Priam's son Lykaon, whom he had captured in a former raid and who had been ransomed. Lykaon is helpless, without armor, and throws himself upon Achilles' mercy, clasping him around the knees. There is a long and reasonable supplication, but Achilles is blind to all reason. Patroklos is dead, why should this lesser man be alive? Achilles kills him even as he is begging for his life and throws him into the river.

Then Achilles meets Asteropaios, who is kin (through his father) to the river Axios. Asteropaios makes his boast and hurls two spears at once: he is ambidextrous. One strikes the shield and is deflected, the other draws blood from Achilles' arm. Achilles then kills him and boasts that the children of Zeus (like

himself) are stronger than the children of rivers. He then kills
the companions of Asteropaios. But while he is at this new
slaughter, the river Xanthos rises up and speaks.

The river is angry that Achilles has killed so many and
desecrated his waters with such carnage. Achilles leaps in the
river to fight the river-god. He is all but overwhelmed; even
when he escapes to the land, The river follows him, washing
the land from beneath his feet as he tries to run. Hephaistos
must come and rescue him.

COMMENTARY: In this epic battle of Fire and Water there is
                    symbolized one of the great themes of the
poem: the two powers of the war, the sea which brought
the Greeks and the destructive fire that will bring down
Troy. These elements have no strict interpretation in
themselves; they are the cosmic presences in which and
with which Homer sees the acting out of the destiny of
the poem. The Greeks are a water people, living on islands and moving in ships. Achilles' mother is of the
ocean. The Greeks' worst moment (Books XI-XV) is
when they are caught between fire and water. War is itself throughout the poem compared to fire. Homer's
symbols tend to be mute, but never puzzling. Fire and
water are irreconcilable, and the poem is about irreconcilable forces in mankind.

The battle of Xanthos and Hephaistos belongs
to the world of fairy tale, an element that Homer uses
sparingly, but which was obviously a part of the tradition in which he works. With the note of fantasy thus set,
the rest of the book moves wholly into the ludicrous and
the comic, to sink to reality again with the spectacle of
Achilles madly chasing a phantom whom he thinks to
be the warrior Agenor but who is Apollo playing a trick
on him.

The ludicrous battle of the gods opens with Homer telling
us that Zeus is vastly amused by his immortals on the battlefield and sits on Olympos laughing at them.

First Athena hits Ares and knocks him seven acres. She
then hits Aphrodite in the breasts, and Aphrodite faints. Apollo
and Poseidon have an argument, and Apollo declines to fight.

Hera beats up Artemis, who spills her arrows and runs away crying. Hermes declines to fight with Leto, on the grounds that he will be beaten and never hear the last of it on Olympos. Artemis arrives indignant before Zeus, to claim justice, and he laughs at her. The gods have made such a preposterous mess of their warriorship that they go back to Olympos, some triumphant, some fuming with anger. Apollo remains to protect Troy.

The Greeks, however, have the upper hand in the human war, and the Trojans retreat within the city. Agenor chooses to remain outside and fight Achilles. He makes an ineffectual spearcast, and as Achilles is about to retaliate, Apollo puts a mist around him and returns him to Troy. Apollo takes on the image of Agenor and runs away, subtly getting Achilles away from the gates so that the Trojans can get to safety.

COMMENTARY: The comic scenes of the gods fighting have annoyed many modern critics, who feel that the *Iliad* is a sober tragedy (as it is, and one of the greatest in the world) and that comic scenes, especially ones of such buffoonery, are aesthetically wrong. Perhaps. What we must try to understand is the Greek attitude, the spirit in which the scenes were conceived and appreciated. For one thing, the *Iliad* is literature, not a religious scripture. However pious a Greek might be toward his gods, he was apparently willing to let them be glorious fools in his literature. Again, the Homeric poems were composed for a known audience, and we can see that it was an audience that was willing to be transported suddenly from grief to silliness, from the sublime to the ridiculous.

The gods are comic, to themselves and to mortals, for the simple reason that immortality precludes seriousness. All of the serious depths of human thought come from the fact that we are going to die. We love, knowing that what we love is going to die. Our every action and attitude is hedged in by death. Not so the gods; eternity is before them. All the forces that have shaped humanity are absent from the lives of the gods, or are there but without the consequences exacted of mankind.

There is another reason we might suggest for the fantastic action of this book. We are but five books from the end, and those five books are tragic. Most of what has gone before has been tragic. Perhaps Homer felt that the long somber design needed an element of tomfoolery here before the worst—not so much comic relief (which implies a break in continuity, a distraction) as a healthy willingness to play with his grand material, to create a *fantasia* (as in music) before he resolves his themes in human grief again.

Note the balance in the book between ruthlessness and terror (Achilles' slaughter in the river) and frivolity and silliness (the comic battle of the gods). These are in turn fitted into two transitional modes which are partly comic, partly serious: the surrealistic battle of the river and Achilles (which makes a transition from the bloody slaughter to the absurd slapstick of the gods) and Achilles chasing the phantom of Agenor (which makes a transition from the playfulness of the gods back to the seriousness of the human battle).

Book XXII: The Book of Hektor's Death

Inside the city the Trojans, who had "run like frightened deer," gasp and dry their sweat. Apollo has led Achilles far enough away for their safe retreat, and stops and taunts him and discloses himself. Chagrined, Achilles runs back to Troy "like a racehorse." Priam, watching on the wall, is the first to see him: he seems to Priam to be as bright as the star called Orion's Dog (remember that his armor is supernatural, and would be brighter than any other armor). Hektor is still outside the wall, waiting to duel with Achilles. Priam tries to dissuade him, for so many of his fifty sons have died at Achilles' hands. "Even now I cannot see Lykaon and Polydoros"—both are dead and both killed by Achilles (Books XX and XXI) though Priam does not yet know it. Priam pleads that the safety of the women of Troy depends on Hektor and that it is wrong for him to throw his life away. He asks Hektor to take pity on him in his old age, for he cannot fight, and if Hektor dies the old men will have to fight. Hekabe, Hektor's mother, bares her bosom, asking him to take pity on her, who will be sold into slavery if the city falls.

But Hektor will not relent. He stands firm, waiting for Achilles. He is not, however, wholly convinced that he is doing right. He feels that the people will say he was foolhardy, that he was overconfident in his strength and caused the fall of Troy out of vanity. Yet he is ashamed not to fight. He knows that he cannot bargain with Achilles: "one might as well talk to a tree or a rock." He cannot entreat him with soft words. There is no treasure, not even the return of Helen, that can tempt Achilles. For this duel is complex: it is both public and personal. It has to do with Patroklos, not, as the war at large does, with the rape of Helen.

But as Achilles comes up to him, Hektor uncontrollably, shamefully, frantically runs away. "A great man ran away," Homer says, "but a greater one by far ran after him."

He did not know that he was going to run. He as little suspected it of himself as Achilles, who knows nothing of fear, expected it of him. They are both surprised. They were like runners running for a prize, Homer says. And the prize was Hektor's life.

COMMENTARY: Nothing in Homer's two epics is so pitiful, or so human, as Hektor's flight.

The terror of this scene is immense. To bolt and run on a battlefield far from home is one thing; one's shame could be minimized by distance and by its being heard about rather than seen. To run before one's parents, and across the familiarity of one's own yard, is another. To drive home the pity of *where* Hektor is running, Homer carefully describes the place where the women wash their clothes, and uses this as a marker to count the number of times Hektor runs around the wall. It is, Homer says, as in a dream, when one runs and cannot escape one's pursuer: one of the psychologically constant situations of human dreams, and a feeling of utter helplessness that we have all experienced.

The fourth time around, Zeus weighs in his scales the destinies of the two men. It is, the scales show, Hektor's death day, and Apollo, who has been giving him strength, gives him up to his fate.

Deiphobos (as Hektor thinks, but it is really Athena) comes to help him, and he stops and faces his enemy. Hektor

regains his dignity and poise. He offers not to despoil Achilles'
body after death if Achilles will not despoil his, but turn it
over to his people for a proper burial. Achilles replies that
there are no understandings between men and lions.

Achilles throws first, and Hektor avoids the cast. Pallas
makes Achilles' spear return to him. Hektor throws; his spear
bounces back from the magic shield. He calls to Deiphobos,
who he thinks is behind him, to hand him another spear. But
there is no Deiphobos, and never was. It was a phantom that
had beguiled him into taking a stand.

Hektor knows that this is the moment of his death, but he
will not die without a fight. He draws his sword, and makes
a plunge "like an eagle." Achilles knows Hektor's armor well,
since it is his own (stripped from Patroklos); he knows precisely
where he can thrust his spear—between the breastplate and the
collar. As the spear sinks in, Achilles says that he will feed his
body to the dogs while he is giving Patroklos a great funeral.
He wishes that his fury were such that he might eat Hektor
raw.

Dying, Hektor prophesies Achilles' death. Paris will shoot
him from the Skaian Gate. Hektor's soul goes mourning to
Hades, "leaving the young body and the manliness behind."
Achilles is still shouting, "Die!" as the body grows cold.

Achilles lashes the body (piercing the ankles at the heel)
by leather thongs to his chariot and drags the body around
the Trojan walls. A wail of lamentation rises from the city.
Hekabe rends her hair. Hektor's wife, Andromakhe, is at her
weaving during the duel and knows nothing of it. She has just
ordered water to be heated for Hektor's bath when she hears
the great cry go up. She arrives at the wall in time to see the
last lap of the circling, when Achilles turns away and drags the
body to the Greek ships.

The book ends with Andromakhe's lament. She compares
their two destinies, both ill-starred. She weeps for the future
of their child (as she will again at the very end of the epic).
She remembers all the fine clothes she has laid away for him,
some of which would be fitting for burial raiment, but these
she will throw in the fire, for she knows that the dogs will eat
Hektor. He must have for burial raiment only the honor that

the Trojans, men and women, all, have always given him, their protector. "Thus she spoke, weeping, and the women mourned with her."

COMMENTARY: Hektor's death is not, as we might have expected, staged like all the other deaths in the middle of a battle, but after a battle, with the two men alone, except for the Trojans watching from their wall and the Greeks watching at a distance from the plain.

The first duel of the epic (Book III) was between Paris, the abductor of Helen, and Menelaos, Helen's husband. They might well have dueled outside the context of a war, for in one sense what became the war was a personal matter between Menelaos and Paris. In an ordered world, however, all misbehavior amplifies and disorders, in chain reaction, the order around it. Paris and Menelaos are the symbols of the disordering forces; the war itself is the disorder, and Hektor and Achilles are very far away indeed from the personal feud of Menelaos and Paris when they face each other. One of the clearest lessons of the *Iliad* is that force grows and accelerates once it is released. The context in which it was first released tends to become irrelevant. It is just and noble that Hektor defend his city, and the larger shape of his heroism does not disappear when he faces Achilles, who has come not to take Troy but to revenge Patroklos' death. Hektor dies, after all, in a personal feud, not in the Trojan War. The irony of this leads us back to the first duel, which is here repeated with other actors, and this time conclusively. There could be no more eloquent demonstration by an artist of the reverberations of the disorder of war. Hektor's death is cruel, pitiful, and tragic. That he ran from Achilles at first emphasizes the indecision in his mind of the nature of the duel. Should he not, as his father and mother pleaded, see Troy as his first duty? Achilles did not challenge on behalf of the Greeks and Menelaos' pursuit of his wife; Achilles came on behalf of Achilles. His hatred had become distinct from the collective anger of the two armies.

The tragedy is not yet over. As the book closes, Hektor's body is being dragged to the ships in total dishonor, and Patroklos' body awaits all the honor that the

Greeks can give it. The rest of the poem will be concerned with the struggles of love and piety to honor those noble bodies.

Book XXIII: The Book of The Funeral Games

This book is concerned with the funeral of Patroklos and the ritual contests with which the Greeks celebrated the death of a hero. When the Myrmidons return from the plain (where they watched Achilles kill Hektor), they ride three times around Patroklos' body, weeping—some two hundred chariots driving past the bier on the beach. Achilles throws himself upon the corpse once again, and tells it that he has brought back the slain and insulted body of Hektor, and twelve young Trojans to be slain.

There is a feast of all the Greeks which Achilles attends covered with the filth and gore of battle, for he will not wash until Patroklos is buried. Achilles sleeps indifferently on the beach, half dead with fatigue and grief. Here the ghost of Patroklos comes to him.

You sleep, Achilles, and you have forgotten me.

A chilling and unexpected accusation from Patroklos' ghost! Patroklos is in that realm of non-being between the living and the dead; he cannot enter Hades until his body has been burned and the ashes put to rest. Achilles attempts to embrace the ghost, and fails, and Patroklos sinks "like mist" into the ground.

Achilles hastens to fulfill the rites as soon as dawn shows. Woodsmen chop enough wood for a pyre, and the Greek army files past the body, laying on it their hair which they have cut off in grief. The body is wrapped in the fat of oxen. Four horses, two dogs, and twelve Trojans are slain and placed on the bier. But the fire will not catch, and there has to be a supplication to the winds.

Achilles mourns "as a father for his son" as the flames consume Patroklos. He lies, weeping, close by the fire. It burns all night, and Achilles falls asleep before it is entirely burnt out. The last of the fire is put out with wine.

Hektor's body lies close by: preserved by the gods from rotting, and is even healed of its wounds.

Agamemnon and Achilles talk together about a tomb (a rough one is to be built, and later a better one, to hold Achilles as well). They have not spoken a friendly word (except the tense exchange of apologies) in the entire poem.

COMMENTARY: Homer is subtly drawing together all the order that had collapsed just as the poem began. When, from the first line of the epic, we began to see the heroic world of the Greek warriors, that world was in turmoil, at cross-purposes. Troy, by contrast, maintained its order. Now the opposite is true. Troy is in confusion; and order —at tragic price—has returned to the Greek army. The games that follow are as much a symbol of the restored Greek order as a celebration of Patroklos' memory.

The word *hero* meant primarily a military and atheletic figure who was his people's defender. "The wall of his people" is a common phrase in early Greek literature (and is what the word *hektor* means). All the sports of the Greeks were in fact military training, and the games held at funerals were an assertion of the community that though a hero had fallen the rest of the people were prepared to carry on.

Achilles offers prizes for a series of contests: a horse race, boxing, wrestling, a foot race, a duel with spears, shot putting, archery, and javelin hurling.

The horse race is described at greater length than the other contests, and is filled with dramatic incidents (a bad place in the course, the loss of a whip). Nestor the garrulous gives long instructions to his son Antilokhos. Diomedes wins, though there is, typically, an argument over who did.

Before the next contest Achilles gives Nestor a prize "for the giving of it," since he is too old to enter, and Nestor reminisces at length over the victories of his youth, giving us (as in all his tales of the past) a glimpse of an heroic world.

The boxing match is won by Epeios. Both Aias and Odysseus win the wrestling match (a draw). Odysseus wins the foot race (in which the younger Aias falls into horse dung and is the cause of much laughter). Aias and Diomedes both

win the duel with spears (another draw). Polypoites wins the
shot put (the prize for which is a hunk of pig iron, showing us
the rareness of that metal in Bronze Age Greece).

The archery contest is worthy of Robin Hood. A pigeon is
tied to the mast of a ship. Teukros shoots and hits the string by
which it is tied; Meriones quickly grabs the bow and shoots the
bird itself before it can fly away.

Agamemnon enters the spear-throwing contest and Achilles, with a wonderfully ambiguous gesture, gives him first prize
without the formality of the throwing. Is he afraid of riling the
savage, suspicious temper again, or is he showing that he has
forgotten and forgiven? Both, probably. In any case, it is a
handsome gesture from Achilles, whatever sly insult he meant
by it.

The Greeks are now at peace with themselves.

Book XXIV: The Book of Priam and Achilles

Achilles still rages at the dead Hektor, dragging him
around the tomb every day for twelve days, and weeps for the
dead Patroklos.

On Olympos, Apollo pleads for the return of Hektor's
body to Priam. "Achilles," he says, "has destroyed pity, and lost
all shame from his soul." Achilles has exceeded the limits of
normal revenge; his fury has become morbid, and draws near
to being an obscenity before the gods, and insanity before men.
Zeus, too, pleads for a cessation of the despoliation. Hektor,
he says, was loved by the gods when he was alive. "I, too, loved
him." So Iris is sent to Thetis (she must plummet into the sea
like a fisherman's lead) who is to persuade Achilles to give
over the body. Thetis goes to Achilles, but does not need to
persuade him. He relents immediately; if the gods are frown-
ing, he will give up the body without argument.

As Troy, King Priam has not eaten or slept, and sits with
dung smeared on his face. All Troy mourns for Hektor, whose
body, they imagine, has long since been eaten by dogs.

Iris comes to Priam, tells him that the body is unspoiled,
and that if he offers a ransom for it and goes and begs for it

himself, he can bring it back. The act, however, is unthinkable to Hekabe and the Trojans. A king debase himself before his son's murderer and beg for the body? The king of Troy venture alone into the Greek camp? A Trojan humble himself before a Greek?

But Priam curses his children and prepares to go. Clearly he is mad with grief. He loved three of his sons more than the others, Mestor, Troilos, and Hektor, and now they are all dead. To Hektor, before the duel, Priam had said, "Everything a young man does is decorous," meaning that there is a pliability and natural gracefulness that enhances the good deeds of the young and excuses the bad. But an old man is under a different set of rules: his dignity is all he has, and now (as Priam feared when he was trying to dissuade Hektor from the duel) he must throw that dignity away and go begging among men who hate him and have killed his sons.

Hermes comes down to guide Priam, disguised as a hand-some young man, a Myrmidon who can take Priam to Achilles' hut. Priam crosses the plain alone at night, with only a wagon and its driver to bring back the body. The wagon is piled high with embroidered cloaks and tripods of gold: the ranson. Hermes leads Priam through the guards (whom he puts to sleep) and through the door of Achilles' hut. There he discloses his identity and goes away.

Achilles has just finished supper when Priam enters. It is an electric, highly tragic moment. The old man kneels and clasps Achilles' knees, and kisses the "dangerous hands, the slaughterers of men, that had slain his sons."

"Achilles," he says, "you are like the gods, think of your father, who is old like me." His speech is dignified, restrained, yet straightforward and bluntly truthful. He has come, without any reason except love, to beg for his son's body. Achilles sees the anguish in the old man, and they weep together: Priam for Hektor, Achilles for Patroklos and his father.

Achilles makes the old man eat with him—an act of kindness, but it must have been harder for Priam to eat bread with Hektor's slayer than to have kissed his knees and hands.

The body (which the two never look at together) is

placed in the wagon. Priam lies down to sleep (hidden, so that no Greek can come in unexpectedly and find him), but Hermes gets him up while it is still dark and leads him out again. Achilles has accepted all of the ransom except two cloaks and a shirt, which he dresses Hektor in.

Kassandra (Priam's daughter who will later guess the meaning of the Trojan horse, though no one will believe her) is the first to see the old man returning to Troy. Achilles has granted twelve days of truce for Hektor's funeral.

Three funeral chants end the epic on a somber, dirge-like note: Andromakhe's, Hekabe's, Helen's. Each is an encomium and a farewell, spoken to Hektor.

Andromakhe's is intimate and moving. Hekabe's, sad as is it, ends triumphantly: Hektor's death did not bring Patroklos back to life; thus Achilles' revenge was futile and impotent. Helen's is a tribute to Hektor's good nature, for Hektor was her only friend.

The funeral is held under the threatening shadow of an impending Greek attack. The last line of the poem is unrivaled in its strong simplicity:

Thus they buried Hektor the tamer of horses.

COMMENTARY: The last book of the *Iliad* is a deliberate anti-climax. The end of the epic's action comes when Achilles kills Hektor. The subject of the poem, however, is Achilles' anger, as the first line states, and the story of that anger must carry us to its ultimate resolution, for Hektor's death does not end it so much as feed fuel to it. It is Priam who ends the anger; it is Priam who makes a human being of Achilles again, taking him from the abstract realm of pure action and absolute emotion, states of mind that are akin to madness and delusion.

The world of men is a system of allegiances and therefore of sympathies. When Priam awakes in Achilles the memory of his father and thus makes him understand the claims of Hektor's father, he cools the heat of a raging psychological fever. Achilles partakes of both the divine and the human in his nature. Priam makes him wholly human for the moment. In madness he killed Hektor and desecrated his body; in sanity he gives him back.

The heroic nature was wide, capable of more cruelty than ordinary men, but also capable of larger kindness. In the last book we see the character of Achilles all the way across, from intense cruelty to intense solicitude. There are no half measures in the man.

The scene of Priam's supplication has been equaled for tragic emotion only by the closing scene of Shakespeare's *Lear*. Homer's effect, like Shakespeare's, comes from the particularity of his narration. Nothing is smoothed over, nothing stylized. The illusion of reality is rich and dense, and every detail is radiant with meaning.

CRITICAL ANALYSIS

The "Shape" of The Iliad

The most obvious shape of the *Iliad* is its systematic pulse of action, following the rhythms of charge and retreat, of force and reaction. Its plot moves as the heart beats, expanding and contracting. The two armies alternately have the upper hand. The battles move back and forth across the plain. The Trojans are now on this side, now on that, of their wall. The Greeks attack, and retreat from, the Skaian Gate of Troy. The gods interfere, do not interfere, and interfere again. Looked at this way (as this is but one organization of the poem), we can see that the plot takes its impact from a break in one of the rhythms—Achilles' anger brings the removal of his Myrmidon army from the attacks. After an agonizingly long while (a few days, in point of time, but long enough to unbalance the poise of strategies), Achilles' Myrmidons are unleashed again, and the rhythm is once more normal. It is as if a strong, loud, long cadence in music suddenly were stopped—creating a dramatic pause—and then returned louder and more forceful than before.

The *Iliad* is a masterpiece of design. The more we look at it, the more admirable its strong organization appears. The *chronological* center of the poem is Book X, which describes the two camps at night, before the great battle that forms the *geometric* center of the poem. Here spies from each side steal into the darkness, and the Greek chiefs watch anxiously for the dawn. Because of the cold night air, they dress in animal skins (leopard, lion, wolf). The scene is sinister and dramatic. It is the nature of balanced symmetry to display meaning by position, so we must consider this dark center of the poem at which men are dressed like animals and prowl by night. As the poem begins, the men are snarling at each other. Achilles calls Agamemnon "Dogface!" The last word of the poem is "horsetamer." Consider the implications of such symmetry: Homer is suggesting that men at war (or in the heat of anger) are bestial, whereas civilized man has the power to tame beasts, including the one in his own heart. In many similes Homer compares the warriors to angry beasts.

The period of time encompassed by the *Iliad* is fifty-five days, twenty-seven of which precede the night described in Book X, twenty-seven of which follow. The four days prior to this midpoint are those of the battle which begins with Pandaros' violation of truce made by Paris and Menelaos and ends with the death of Hektor. Four days after the midpoint, the Greeks hold the funeral games for Patroklos. These symmetrically poised moments establish polar opposites: the chaotic *dissolution* of order (anger, war, treachery, disappointment, a broken truce), the *restoration* of order (reconciliation, peace, trust among the Greeks, the fulfillment of religious rites, heroic games).

Cedric Whitman's *Homer and the Heroic Tradition* (see BIBLIOGRAPHY) presents a detailed schema of the geometric pattern of the *Iliad*. Much of the symmetry is strong and obvious and much of it (as Professor Whitman shows) is subtle and hidden. Remember that the design of a work of art has its impact on us whether we are aware of it or not (see CHART, p. 6).

The Literary Achievement

Homer's Style   Every age finds different qualities to admire in Homer—this would seem to be the mark of great literature, that it endures as its beauty and truth are adaptable to the tastes of each generation. In the twentieth century, for example, Ezra Pound has celebrated the *realism* in Homer: the slaughter of the battle scenes is intimate to its smallest gory detail, chariots and ships are described with great technical accuracy. The frequently sustained irony of the paradoxical epithet (the "godlike" Alexander, the "swift-footed" Achilles in situations where they may not be so); the poet's wry, occasionally blasphemous humor as in the rollicking battle of the gods (Book XXI); show Homer, the poet of antiquity, to have skillfully handled those facets of literary art which so preoccupy the "modern" poets.

Matthew Arnold, the English critic (1822-1888), found four qualities in Homer's style: rapidity, a plainness and directness in the evolution of his thought, a plainness and directness in the substance of his thought, and nobility.

By nobility, Arnold meant several things. One is Homer's command of the emotions he evokes. He is never at a loss with a human emotion, and describes with perfect understanding such divergent emotions as Diomedes' battle mania, the fear of Hektor's infant son when Hektor puts on his helmet, Agamemnon's childish selfishness, and Hektor's panic when he runs from Achilles. Ultimately we read literature for what it can tell us about other people, and we therefore justifiably value a writer for how much he knows. Homer knows his entire world, and impartially displays the whole range of the life of man—and of the gods (which for the Greeks was the life of man amplified). Homer describes with equal care the dressing of Hera to seduce Zeus and the brutal carnage of the battlefield.

Homer is never embarrassed by any human emotion. Nowhere in Homer can we find him disapproving of a person acting according to his own nature.

Homer always speaks with an easy fluidity. He is neither wasteful nor stingy with words. He does not point to anything: he shows. Epic poetry was meant to teach as well as to entertain, and Homer's mode of teaching was to establish resemblances, hence the use of *simile* when he wants us to see exactly. The Homeric simile takes something familiar (a farmer recoiling from a snake) and puts it beside something we have not seen (a soldier recoiling from a sudden ambush). We see the two together, and understand the one by means of the other.

The similes can be elaborate (as when the armies are

compared to harvesters or to wood-choppers, and a full picture of peaceful agriculture or forestry is put beside the sword work of a battle) or terse and epigrammatic:

> Even as the generation of leaves, so are those of men *(VI, 146)*

Greek is a language in which a poet can achieve extraordinary effects, and Homer has many unforgettable lines in which he has made the words speak with great eloquence. For example:

> dana de klang-ga genet argire-oy-o bi-oy-o *(I,49)*

The line describes Apollo shooting an arrow from his bronze bow: familiar with the Greek or not, the listener can hear the clang of the released string, and its quivering. Homer is a master of onomatopoeia (imitative sound) and uses it to powerful effect; few translators have succeeded in carrying this quality across the language barrier.

Homer is always concrete: he talks in terms of things rather than abstractions. It was, however, in the nature of his world to assign human qualities to objects. A sword was made of "pitiless bronze."

The *Iliad* is both a well integrated and an almost infinitely rich panorama of the Greek world. This is achieved in several ways. One is the insertion of short myths of gods and men; for example, the tale of Meleagros that Phoinix tells to Achilles, or Agamemnon's tale of the birth of Herakles. Another is Homer's habit of telling us something of every man's native land and family, so that vistas are opened in the plot even in the thickest battles. Another is the alternation of the action between the "heavenly" Olympos or Mount Ida and the earth. Another is such a device as the catalogues of the Greeks and the Trojan allies, in which Homer includes a thumbnail geography of Greece, the islands, and Asia Minor.

Homer's attention is versatile. It moves everywhere with equal ease, so that it makes the most of everything it comes upon. When the physician Makhaon is wounded, old Nestor goes into the battle to rescue him. Makhaon is wounded because Homer wants all the chief Greek warriors to be incapacitated at once, to strengthen Patroklos' plea that Achilles come back into the war. Nestor takes Makhaon to his hut, to tend to his wounds and offer him a meal. The occasion, we see, is carefully staged, for Patroklos will show up, and Nestor will plant the hint that he persuade Achilles. But the scene is more than a device of the plot; Homer describes everything: the wine, the food, the talk, the servants. Nor are such tableaus atypical. When the Russian novelist Tolstoy attempted to describe the Napoleonic wars with a Homeric thoroughness in his novel *War and Peace*, he required a thousand pages more than Homer (1,350 as against the 350 pages of Homer in Greek). Very few artists have ever achieved Homer's precision and compression.

Homer's Way of Seeing The World

Homer's peculiar ability to satisfy practically all tastes may be attributed to his wonderfully generous mind. He lived, not in the age he describes, but in a commercial and bureaucratic world. So in a sense he was describing a world (the times of Mycenae, Knossos, and Pylos as world powers) that never was just the way he sought to make it. This does not make his great generosity any the less real or sincere.

By generosity we mean the view whereby everything and everybody has its place in a world that the poet accepts. He never condemns the actions that are native to a place or a people. The Aiolians in the *Odyssey*, for instance, are incestuous (and very happy, Homer adds); the Laistrygonians have always been and probably always will be cannibals; that's the affair of the Laistrygonians. To Homer the Trojans are as admirable a people as the Greeks. There are no ideologies in the *Iliad;* there is no "enemy." Homer is completely impartial. He is a very moral man, a religious man if you will, and yet it was the nature of his religion to accept the world in its large diversity. He is not shocked by the nature of things or the behavior of the gods. This is not to say that he does not study deeply the consequences of misbehavior; the *Iliad* is a poem of war and Homer knows that war is a kind of plague or contagious madness. He knows what the world ought to be, and what the true nature of man is.

Two modern writers, Simone Weil and Rachel Bespaloff, have said that the real hero of the *Iliad* is *force;* that it is, above all other matters in the poem (love, friendship, loyalty, courage), the raw power of the sword, the chariot, the spear. Hektor's spear is sixteen feet long and its tempered bronze point could pierce an armored man through. There is also the force of fire, mentioned everywhere in the poem (because Troy will eventually burn). There is the force of the human body. Aias, Hektor, and Achilles are built like bulls, rock-hard of muscle and as lithe as leopards. For the Greeks the human body was a machine to be trained to its utmost endurance to kill. If there is a shade of difference between Trojan and Greek that will tilt the balance against the Trojan, it is the softness of the Trojan as we see it in Pandaros the archer and Alexandros, who will kill Achilles with an arrow, not a spear.

The *Iliad* very nearly has two protagonists: Achilles and Hektor. That is, Achilles is clearly the protagonist, for it is his story, not Hektor's. Yet Hektor is as large a character and, to our eyes, is more noble, certainly a more stable and admirable man. If the poem were about peace, Hektor might well be the protagonist. But it is a poem of war, and war to Homer is one man's anger extended to whole peoples and cities. And anger is self-destructive. No one ever wins a war; the victor is as maimed, and has lost as much, as the vanquished. Achilles asks to be buried with Patroklos "by whoever of you is left at that time." War has only one medium: death. There is as much reason for saying that the hero of the *Iliad* is death as for saying that it is force. Every death in the epic stops the narrative for however little, so that we can know the importance of the life that is lost. The triumph—tragic triumph—of the poem is that two men, Priam and Achilles, cease for a single hour to be the agents of death, and speak together of the claims of life, of loyalty to parents, of grief. In that moment the anger of Achilles is suspended. Only death can quell it.

CHARACTER ANALYSIS

There are over 250 names of importance in the *Iliad;* each character is memorable in one way or another. Those discussed below are the more significant, complex, or spectacular. Others that cannot go without mention will be found in the GLOSSARY, "Mortals, Gods, Goddesses, and Places, in the *Iliad.*."

The Greeks

Achilles   Protagonist of the *Iliad*. The wrath of Achilles is the subject of the epic, as the opening line says. The structure of the epic is determined by the direction of that wrath: first toward Agamemnon, who has cheated and insulted Achilles, and then toward Hektor, who has killed Achilles' friend in battle. The two destructive fits of anger begin and end the action of the epic, but they do not define entirely the character of Achilles. The two angers are sharply different: the quarrel with Agamemnon discloses a childish, primitive selfishness that is nevertheless condoned by the code of Greek behavior. The second springs from love. So complex, however, is Achilles' character, that we can see that the second anger is also rooted in Achilles' selfishness, for Patroklos was ambiguously many things to Achilles—devoted friend, fellow warrior, servant, and psychological opposite whose unselfish disposition complemented Achilles' arrogance and impatience with other people. Patroklos was also something like Briseis, the prize girl, and Hektor's killing Patroklos is parallel to Agamemnon's claiming Briseis. Achilles loves things and people for the honor they give him. He is with the Greek forces to win honor and prizes for himself, not primarily to be an ally to Agamemnon and Menelaos. It is his fate to lose all that he loves, and to have to fight for them after he has lost them and cannot reclaim them.

Achilles is a tragic figure, and for the Greeks tragedy was the deepening (or awakening) of understanding through a calamity that changes one's relationship to the world. Achilles is reconciled to Agamemnon, and he is, to his surprise, reconciled in a sense to Hektor. When Hektor, before his death, asks for an agreement that neither combatant will despoil the other's body but return it for decent burial, Achilles refuses, saying that the lion makes no pacts. Yet Achilles does return Hektor's body once his grief for Patroklos has made him understand the claims of other people's grief (a quality of manhood rather than of lions). He also learns sympathy when Priam makes him understand how Achilles' father, Peleus, will feel when he, too, is dead in battle.

Ultimately Achilles is a character of great nobility, not only for the generosity with which he releases others from the cruelty of his anger but also because he accepts the fate that he has known all along: that he has the choice of winning glory and dying young, or of living to an inglorious old age. He does not question that fate when he goes to avenge Patroklos, for here love has canceled selfishness, though he mentions the fate as one of his reasons for remaining firm in his resolve to bring disgrace on Agamemnon.

In Achilles we see the maturity of a man who, from birth, was used to taking admiration for granted, who remained a child at heart, with all of a child's claims to attention and prerogatives. At the beginning of the *Iliad* he is a prince among men, haughty and arrogant, a lucky man accomplished in war and rich in possessions and friends, and with the whole attention of his mind directed toward his own aggrandizement and luxury. When the *Iliad* closes he is also a wise man, for he has learned pity and the larger scope of the heart's understanding wherein the suffering of others has dissolved both his anger and his selfishness.

Agamemnon   He is the leader of the forces by right of wealth and royal position. As a general he ranks low, and for all his self-importance he has no genius for command. As a man he is proud, surly, a bit stupid, and arrogant. His selfishness is greater than Achilles'. There is much of the typical Greek peasant in him: he is suspicious, headstrong, maudlin in emotion and blustering when he wants his way. One imagines him as a tall, black-bearded man with shifty eyes, haughty as a horse and about as intelligent.

Aias, Son of Telemon   He is the supreme hoplite (fully armored foot soldier, whose weapon is the long spear) and the model soldier that military academies still think of as the essence of the faithful, tough, obedient infantryman. He is of enormous physique: his name has become synonymous with strength. He is slow of wit, blunt, and honest. He moves "like a wall." With his namesake, Aias son of Oileus, and his half-brother, Teukros, he is a formidable obstacle to the enemy.

Antilokhos   The son of Nestor; he brings the news of Patroklos' death to Achilles, and later takes part in the chariot race in the funeral games. He is a young Greek, but an experienced and capable warrior.

Helen   She was the most beautiful woman in the world, the daughter of Leda and Zeus; and her two lovers, the

Spartan Menelaos and the Trojan Paris represented the extremes of human conduct. She is not happy to be, in effect, the slave of Aphrodite. She is not at home in Troy; her beauty gives her no real pleasure. Nowhere does Homer offer moral condemnation of her: to be fought over has made her more of an object than a human being; she is merely beautiful. Helen is both Trojan and Greek; whichever way the victory falls, she is both winner and loser.

Menelaos   Considering that Helen is his wife, for whose reclamation the war is fought, Menelaos plays a surprisingly small role in the epic. He is usually present in the great battles, but plays a role that could just as well belong to Sarpedon or Aias or Diomedes. Except for his courage there is no particular trait that sets him aside from the others. By making Menelaos no more prominent than the other Greek heroes, Homer adds to the effect that the war has outgrown its nature as a punitive raid to recover Helen and has become a contest of wills and power.

Nestor   The grand old man of the Greek army. He acts as an arbitrator in the quarrels and in assemblies, and his memories of the past serve to deepen the time sense of the epic. He is a superb story teller, though his stories are always a trifle too long, and his advice is charmingly more than anyone might ask for. It is his hint to Patroklos that eventually brings Achilles into the fighting.

Patroklos   Kind, solicitous, handsome, nakedly sincere, and without any ambition except to please his lord Achilles, Patroklos bears in his blameless heart the very kind of innocence that makes him completely vulnerable to the world. There is a clear feeling among the Greeks that if they can contrive to have him killed by the Trojans, they will thereby unleash Achilles. This is not an overt plan, of course, else it could not have worked (indeed, it would have backfired), but even Patroklos seemed to known instinctively that it was what he had to do ("and he, unknowing, innocently asked for his own death").

The Trojans

Aeneas   Son of Aphrodite and the Trojan Ankhises, Aeneas is perhaps more important for his traditional founding of Rome after the fall of Troy, than for his actual role in Homer. His pre-duel speech, however, prior to the encounter with Achilles, is the most interesting and elaborately developed writing of its kind in the *Iliad*.

Andromakhe   Achilles has killed her father and burnt her home; in the course of the *Iliad* Achilles kills her husband. She is a portrait of a good wife and mother, and in her character we see the hopes and disappointments of the ordinary Trojan away from the battlefield. She is the kind of competent, devoted woman one would expect Hektor to have married.

Hektor   Generous, kind, the defender of his people, Hektor is, it seems at first, the opposite of the savage and proud Achilles. Yet the two heroes have much in common: they are both capable of completely dominating the battlefield when the battle madness is upon them. Both are embodiments of the heroic ideal; both are fighting in a war begun by others, and both feel keenly the tragic irrelevance of the war to their destinies. Why should Hektor die because his brother stole another man's wife, and why should Achilles die to reclaim her? Hektor appears in the context of his family always: with his wife and child, with his brothers, with his parents. Even in the defenseless moment of his death he imagines that a friend is nearby to help him. As his name implies (*hektor* means *mainstay*), he is his people's protector and accepts this role without question and without selfishness. He is as close to his father as Achilles is remote from his. Achilles is surrounded by friends *because he needs their adoration;* Hektor is surrounded by his family and friends *because he loves them* and cares for their well-being.

Paris (or Alexandros)   Like his mistress Helen, he does not know whether he belongs wholly to the military discipline of his kinsmen or to the magic realm of Aphrodite, and is confused by the two claims. Hektor thinks him "strange" and the Trojans gossip about his dereliction from battle. He is under the spell of a goddess (or as the Greek language says, he was "enthusiastic"); his mind was not his own. He is a lady's man rather than, like Hektor, a man's man, and if contempt were deadly, the Greeks would have killed him in the first days of the war.

Priam   To our modern eyes he is something of a Persian
           Caliph, with his fifty sons and fifty daughters (not to
mention illegitimate offspring). But there is nothing exotic or
oriental about him otherwise, though he reflects in the close-
ness of his family and in his own integrity the patriarchs of the
Old Testament. His wise kindness is everywhere apparent, especially in his relationship to Hektor, Paris, and Helen. He hates
war and can scarcely bring himself to watch the battles. In the
last book of the epic Homer makes him into one of the greatest
tragic figures of all literature.

The Gods as Characters

"War and Zeus are the same thing," said Herakleitos,
one of the earliest of Greek philosophers (sixth century B.C.)
The pronouncements of Herakleitos are deliberately paradoxical
and condensed, but it seems that he meant, by identifying
Zeus and war, that war is a crisis in which all values are laid
naked and evident. Elsewhere, Herakleitos expands his thought:
"War is the father and the ruler of everything. War shows some
men to be god-like, some to be merely men. War shows who is
free and who is a slave." Again: "War is the normal condition
of men. Out of strife comes justice; all things arise out of strife."
Clearly Herakleitos is identifying *all* striving as a kind of warfare (as we say, "a war against disease" or "a war against
poverty").

Herakleitos' formula, Zeus is war, is perhaps a clue to the
Greek concept of the divine. We might also say, "Aphrodite and
love are the same thing," "Hera and the duties and trials and
happiness of marriage are the same thing," but the original state-
ment has much deeper implication. The early Greek mind sought
embodied examples of its abstractions (indeed, the abstractions
of fifth-century thought arose from the everyday realities). The
gods in Homer's poems are thus concretions (though a few
generations afterwards several philosophers began to feel that
the gods were a bit childish and primitive).

Homer did not invent his gods, of course, and we can
be reasonably sure that his attitude toward them was that of his
audience. They were not the stumbling block to appreciation
that they sometimes are to modern readers.

The Homeric Greek seemed to think of his gods primarily

as protectors and as saviors. That is, cities and enterprises were under the guardianship of a god (as Athens under Athena, the growing of crops under Demeter, the composition of music under Apollo). In their role as saviors the gods could intervene in the course of life, to prevent (or provoke) disaster, for instance. Because of the later Greek drama, where the intervening god was portrayed on stage suspended from a rope on a crane (a *machina*), we have come to call this timely intervention the *deus ex machina,* "the god from the machine." The *Iliad* and the *Odyssey* have many such moments.

Again, the gods served the Greek mind as the reality behind all the motivational impulses: love, hate, inspiration, and so on. Conversely, a god was also the force that countered an impulse, taking away a man's courage, or thwarting his ambition.

From an aesthetic point of view, one of the arguments for the effectiveness of the gods as characters is that they may be seen as caricatures of humanity; their virtues and faults exaggerate those of human beings. If Zeus is wiser than any Greek or Trojan, so Aphrodite when she enters the fighting is sillier and more inept than an earthbound soldier could ever be. The presence of the gods is a kind of counterpoint, as in music; their rhythms, their melody, harmonize with that of humanity, but is the grander theme.

Once we have encountered the depths of Homeric poetry, we cannot imagine the human characters without the gods. Athena becomes the mind of Odysseus; Aphrodite the mind of Helen. The god develops as an ideal, the reservoir of potential, which humanity can merely imitate. The brusque heavy-handedness of Agamemnon is merely a foible *until* we realize it as a counterpoint of, a counterforce against Zeus' omnipotent command of men and gods. Agamemnon attempts to play the role of Zeus; he cannot, however, because he is a man, with a man's limitations. Helen is unhappy precisely because she is not Aphrodite. Aphrodite is pure and eternal; Helen can imitate something of her passion, and has the inclination and the beauty for it, but she is also mortal, a wife (a wife to two men, in fact), a mother, and will someday be old and wrinkled. The gods are the perfection of man. Man, for the Greeks, was at his best an imperfect god. Here is a reversal of the caricature and the caricatured; we see man's aspiration toward a divine idealization (of his own manufacture)—here Homer's counterpoint is the smallness of man, especially in death, as the mighty Hektor, hero in the eyes of his city, god in the eyes of his infant child, brought to a broken, crumpled reality in the dust.

SUGGESTED QUESTIONS AND ANSWERS

1. Why the persistence of the imagery of fire?

Suggestions: A symbol of war, wrath, anger, destruction. There are other meanings. To arrive at them find a passage that mentions fire and discover the relevance of the image to the action. Remember that Troy eventually burns. Note the battle between Hephaistos (fire) and Xanthos (water) in Book XXI.

We must distinguish between the dramatic imagery (men, horses, weapons) and the symbolic imagery. Fire, for instance, is a recurring image and acts as a symbol of violence. The interpolated stories and myths are filled with images of peace (agriculture, childhood, innocence). All of the similes tend to contrast peace and war. Consider the images that have to do with animals.

2. The epic begins with a quarrel and ends with a reconciliation (but not among the same people). Explain the dramatic importance of a reconciliation between Priam and Achilles rather than between Achilles and Agamemnon.

Suggestions: The one quarrel led to and complicated the other. Homer is interested in reverberations and effects rather than causes.

3. Hektor's infant son cries when he sees Hektor in the masked, horsetail-crested helmet. Hektor uncontrollably bolts when he sees Achilles in his divine armor. What does Homer imply here?

Suggestions: The scene of the baby prepares for the panic of Hektor, suggesting that panic arises from the unknown, the awesome. There are also other implications.

4. Argue that pity is the dominant emotion in the *Iliad*.

Suggestion: One might just as well say that hate is the dominant emotion. But pity becomes, as the poem progresses, a force as creates the tragic design. Patroklos introduces pity into the poem (ironically). Pity tames the wrath of Achilles.

5. Discuss the comic treatment of the gods.

Suggestion: A twentieth-century answer might be, "Why not?" but we would be shocked by the discovery of a lost document in which the Hebraic or Christian God played a comic part.) Homer's civilization allowed a god to be the subject of a joke without diminishing his prestige as a deity. The *Iliad* is as much about the gods as about men. There is a great difference, however, between the possible destinies of the two. The action of the poem can only be a passing adventure for the gods, who cannot die and who have seen millions of years of wars before the birth of the human characters in the *Iliad*. The comic acts of the gods are Homer's way of indicating the inconsequential nature of all action as seen by an immortal.

6. Compare Zeus and Agamemnon.

Suggestion: Homer often allows Agamemnon to act out a parody of Zeus' actions. (Look at the councils throughout the poem.) And the more godlike Agamemnon is (predicting the future, laying plans which he thinks are divine), the wronger he is in his judgments. There is a comic as well as a very human interpretation that we can see in this parallel. Homer thereby points up the limitations of human action. Man can imitate but never duplicate the divine mind.
strong as that of the hatred and violence that drives the poem almost to its conclusion. It is pity that resolves the action and

7. Discuss Homer's impartiality.

Suggestion: Homer takes neither Greek nor Trojan side in the war. Nor does he posit a hero or a villain. There is a sense in which either Hektor or Achilles is the "hero" of the poem. Achilles is definitely the protagonist ("first actor") of the poem, and yet Achilles is clearly a focal point around which Homer places an array of characters, so that Achilles is, for most of the poem, more of a catalyst of action than an actor himself. Another way to talk about Homer's impartiality is to note that (like Chaucer, Shakespeare, and Tolstoy) he is more interested in understanding human nature than in condemning or commending it. Homer understands and sympathizes with both Hektor and Achilles, Hera and Helen, Agamemnon and Priam.

8. The *Iliad* as a poem.

The *Iliad* is a long narrative and therefore (to our modern eyes) akin to the novel and the motion picture. But because it is a poem it has contours and a development that is close to the design of the lyric poem (that is, a poem that has a subject which it projects upon our imagination and about which it has something to say). Once we know the poem well, we can hold it in our mind as a single trope of meaning. (The analogy with a symphony may be useful here.) The *Iliad*, if it were a musical composition, would begin in strident turbulence and proceed to strong and stormy passages. Then there would be a particularly fierce crescendo (the death of Patroklos) and an ominous quiet. The turbulence would return, but it would be a different theme (the entry of Achilles into battle), and this too would move toward a great turbulence and climax (the death of Hektor). The rest of the composition would be slow and melancholy, but with the dignity of tragedy.

RESEARCH AREAS

1. The character of Achilles.

Suggestions: Note Achilles' dependence on Phoinix (as a child) and on Patroklos. Study carefully the reasons he gives to the embassy (Book IX) for not entering the battle. Note his relationship to Thetis. His character is both noble and weak, mature and childish.

Compare and contrast the two occasions of his anger, his motivations, and the resolutions. How are the two angers related? Note how the gods react to each.

2. The character of Hektor.

Suggestions: Compare the eulogies at his funeral with the scenes in which he appears with the speakers of the eulogies. Note that the funeral speeches characterize him as husband and father, son, and friend.

3. The character of Helen.

Suggestions: Note her relationship with Aphrodite, Paris, Menelaos, and Hektor. Try to say just what her moral dilemma is.

4. The participation of the gods in the war.

Suggestions: Ask yourself if the interference of the gods is ultimately beneficial to mankind, or detrimental. Note how Homer suggests that the gods cannot be wholly serious in their interest in mankind (hence the comic scenes of their inept and ludicrous fighting). How does Zeus differ from the other gods in his attitude toward the war?

5. The rhythms of the plot.

Suggestions: Note that two rhythmic patterns are operative: the larger one of the war (charge and retreat, chaos and order, dispersal and rally) and the smaller (but more immediately important) one of Achilles' withdrawal and re-entry. At what point of crisis do the two patterns coincide?

6. The interpolated stories.

Suggestions: Choose one or several and show the interaction of meaning between the story and the plot of the epic. Why, for instance, does Phoinix tell Achilles the tale of Meleagros (Book IX)? Why does Aeneas, when he faces Achilles in a duel, talk for so long about his ancestry?

7. The funeral games.

Suggestions: Compare the morale of the Greeks in the games with their spirit on the battlefield. Select details that show the friendliness and congenial rivalry of the Greeks among themselves. Note how Nestor gives too much advice to Antilokhos. Why does Achilles give a prize to Agamemnon and waive the contest? What is the importance of the games to the structure of the epic?

8. Rachel Bespaloff (see BIBLIOGRAPHY) suggests that there is a parallelism between Andromakhe and Hera (as there is between Zeus and Hektor), Helen and Aphrodite, Thetis and Pallas Athena. Study these parallels and say what meaning Homer derives from them.

Suggestions: One side of each parallel is human, the other divine, except, of course, Thetis and Pallas. Andromakhe, Helen, and Thetis are tragic figures, because their love is real rather than occasional. Hera, Aphrodite, and Pallas are immortal, and yet their attempts to help are frequently ineffectual. Note the system of selfish and unselfish motivations in this pattern.

BIBLIOGRAPHY

A Note on the Translations

The first English translation, that which inspired Keats' famous sonnet ("Much have I travell'd in the realms of gold . . ."), is Chapman's *Iliad* of 1611. A second English version of historical importance is Alexander Pope's rhymed-couplet translation of 1718. Both Chapman and Pope reflect the tastes of their respective ages, and this is as it should be. Each new age requires its own translation of the classics.

The best translation to date for the English reader is that of Richmond Lattimore (U. of Chicago Press, 1951), an accurate, clear, and highly readable translation into verse. The English poet Christopher Logue has recently rendered parts of the *Iliad* into brilliant poetic paraphrase: the account of Achilles' going into the battle is published under the title "Pax" in the classical journal *Arion*, vol. II, No. 4 (Winter, 1963); the death of Patroklos, *Patrocleia of Homer: A New Version by Christopher Logue* (U. of Michigan Press, 1963). Other translations, readable and faithful to the text, are those of William Cowper, Sir William Marris, A. T. Murray, E. V. Rieu, Ennis Rees, and Samuel Butler.

Critical Studies

Bespaloff, Rachel. *On the Iliad.* New York, 1947 (paperback edition, 1962). A short, intensely written study of the characters and the theme of force. One of the best books ever written about Homer.

——————. *Tradition and Design in the Iliad.* Oxford, 1930. Discusses the *Iliad* in relation to other epics and to oral tradition.

Bowra, C. M. *Heroic Poetry.* London, 1952. A useful comparative study of the epic poetry genre.

Sheppard, J. T. *The Pattern of the Iliad.* London, 1922. A study of the symmetry of the poem, together with an analysis of the shield of Achilles as symbol.

Weil, Simone. *The Iliad, or The Poem of Force.* Lebanon, Pennsylvania, 1945. An essay, more philosophical than literary, on the meaning of the poem; written during the Occupation in France.

Whitman, Cedric. *Homer and the Heroic Tradition*. Cambridge, 1958. A full discussion of many Homeric themes by a major scholar. Professor Whitman has made a minutely detailed study of the geometric structure of the *Iliad*. Highly recommended for students of Homer, interested especially in the structure and imagery (especially that of fire) of the *Iliad*.

Other Standard Works and Related Studies

Allen, T. W. *Homer, Origins and Transmission*. 1924.

Alsop, Joseph. *From the Silent Earth: A Report on the Greek Bronze Age*. New York, 1964. A recent, readable, profusely illustrated account of the excavations at Troy, Pylos, Knossos, and Mycenae. Together with the latest interpretations of the findings. The book includes a long interview with the archaeologist Carl Blegen.

Auerbach, E. *Mimesis*. Princeton, 1953. Chapter One offers an enlightening comparison of the Homeric style with that of the Old Testament; to be used carefully however as it tends toward some over-simplification.

Bassett, S. E. *The Poetry of Homer*. Berkeley, California, 1938. A useful general study.

Carpenter, Rhys. *Folk Tale, Fiction and Saga in the Homeric Epics*. Berkeley, California, 1958. A controversial and fascinating work.

Chadwick, John. *The Decipherment of Linear B*. New York, 1958. The story of Michael Ventris's decoding of the Knossan Greek script first discovered by Sir Arthur Evans at the turn of the century. Chadwick was Ventris's collaborator; a book about the discovery that has caused all ancient history to be seen in a new light.

De Coulanges, Numa Denis Fustel. *The Ancient City*. New York, 1956 (original edition, 1864). This classic study of the organization of ancient Mediterranean societies, especially the city state, remains the definitive description of the Greek world. To read this book is to understand what it must have felt like to live in a world of the intricate, pervasive Greek religion, and the laws that Homer took to be the nature of the universe.

Finley, M. I. *The World of Odysseus.* New York, 1959. This clearly written paperback is a discussion of the manners, morals, laws, customs, in short, the culture that Homer describes. It is both historical and interpretive.

Germain, Gabriel. *Homer.* New York, 1960. A charming, richly illustrated paperback essay on Homer and Homeric times. Translated from the French. One of the best introductions to the subject ever written. Highly recommended for students just beginning the study of Homer who will profit by many illustrations and much background.

Harrison, Jane. *Prolegomena to the Study of Greek Religion.* Cambridge, 1903. A pioneer study of Greek rites, by a disciple of Sir James Frazer (whose *The Golden Bough,* now out of date, was the first great anthropological study of pagan religions). Miss Harrison can tell the student much about the nature of the gods and the meaning of the Greek festivals and rites. The interested student will want to read also Miss Harrison's *Themis,* an expansion of the same subject (New York, 1962).

Kerenyi, Carl. *The Gods of the Greeks.* London, 1951. A more systematic study than the following, describing the organization of religious systems rather than a philosophical interpretation.

_____. *The Religion of the Greeks and Romans.* New York, 1962. A lucid study of what the religions meant, how they worked in their societies. An important book in that it carefully establishes the kind of piety the ancients felt toward their gods and the world.

Kitto, H. D. F. *The Greeks.* Baltimore, 1951. An excellent short book on the culture and art of the ancient Greeks.

Lord, Albert B. *The Singer of Tales.* New York, 1965. An account of research by Lord and Milman Parry on the techniques of oral composition of epic poetry.

Marinatos, S. and M. Hirmer. *Crete and Mycenae.* New York, 1960. Useful for its excellent photography of Minoan and Mycenaean art and architecture.

Murray, Gilbert. *The Rise of the Greek Epic.* (4th ed.), Oxford,

1934. Murray wrote under the influence of folklorist theories now largely out-moded; offers, however, enlightening literary insights into the discipline of epic study.

Myres, J. L. *Who Were the Greeks?* Berkeley, California, 1930. Contains a study of the form of the *Iliad*.

Onians, R. B. *The Origins of European Thought*. Cambridge, 1951. An advanced book, but astounding in its penetration of ancient physiology and psychology. Homer's concept of the body, the mind, of time, of fate, of the gods, and so on. The student curious about the distance between his own and Homer's concept of the nature of things is urged strongly to look into this extraordinary study.

Palmer, Leonard R. *Mycenaeans and Minoans*. New York, 1963. The new light thrown on Bronze Age history by the decipherment of the Linear B Tablets. Reads like a detective story.

Scott, J. A. *The Unity of Homer*. 1921.

Vermeule, Emily. *Greece in the Bronze Age*. Chicago, 1964. A scholarly but clear book which makes many aspects of the Mycenaean Age in Greece very vivid.

Wace, A. J. B. and F. H. Stubbings, eds. *A Companion to Homer*. New York, 1963. This large volume is the most up-to-date gathering of Homeric materials available, covering the critical, linguistic, and archaeological areas of study. It is a scholar's book, but clear, readable and concise even to the casual student.

Zimmern, Alfred. *The Greek Commonwealth*. New York, 1911. The classic study of the economy and everyday life of the Greeks, and of their forms of government.

GLOSSARY

Mortals, Gods, Goddesses,
and Places in the Iliad

Achaeans—a term used generally to refer to the Greeks.

Achilles—the greatest of the Greek warriors, he was the youngest of seven sons born to the sea-nymph Thetis and Peleus (for which reason he was also called *Pelades*). Legend had it that Achilles' mother had made him invulnerable by dipping him into the river Styx; the heel by which she held him was his only vulnerable spot. In the aftermath of the *Iliad*, he is slain by an arrow shot by Paris and guided to the heel by Apollo. Achilles' common epithets are "swift-footed," "godlike," "sacker-of-cities." (See CHARACTER ANALYSIS.)

Aneas—See CHARACTER ANALYSIS, "Trojans."

Agamemnon—the brother of Menelaus and son of Atreus, he is King of Mycenae and the commander of the Greek forces (See CHARACTER ANALYSIS). Prior to the Greek expedition to Troy, Agamemnon had sacrificed his daughter Iphigenia to appease the goddess Artemis (one of whose stags he had slain) in order that Artemis might quiet the storms that made sailing impossible. In the aftermath of the *Iliad*, Agamemnon was one of the few Greek warriors who got home safely and quickly, taking with him the prophetess, and daughter of Priam, Kassandra. In the fifth-century tragedy by Aeschylus, he is slain by his wife Klaitemnestra for his sacrifice of their daughter ten years earlier.

Aias—chief Greek warrior, second only to Achilles.

Alastor—(a) a leader of the Pylians, (b) father of Tros (for whom the Troad was named), (c) a Lycian slain by Odysseus.

Alexandros—Paris (see CHARACTER ANALYSIS, "Trojans"), one of Priam's fifty sons.

Andromakhe—wife of Hektor (see CHARACTER ANALYSIS, "Trojans").

Antenor—Trojan counselor, prominent citizen, the father of many fallen Trojan warriors.

Antilokhos—son of Nestor (See CHARACTER ANALYSIS, "Greeks").

Antiphos—(a) a Greek leader, (b) a Trojan ally, leader of the Maeonians, (c) a son of Priam, captured and released by Achilles but later slain by Agamemnon in Book XI.

Aphrodite—Goddess of love and beauty, she was held to have been
born in the sea from the sperm of Uranus' severed testicles when
Kronos emasculated his father. Homer does not seem to know about
her son Eros (Cupid) or her daughter Peitho ("Seduction"). Because she is the mother of the mortal Aeneas, son of Ankhises, she
takes the Trojan side in the war. She is a charmingly ineffective
warrioress, and Homer creates many comic scenes of her attempts
to do battle. Her true skill is managing "the secret delights of
love" (as Zeus says), so that her two prominent triumphs are the
spiriting away of Paris from battle to the bed of Helen and Hera's
seduction of Zeus so that Poseidon can have a free hand in the
war while Zeus isn't watching. She is the wife of Hephaistos in
the *Odyssey* and in later myth, and also in the *Iliad*, as Kharis ("The
Graceful One") is another of her many names. As might be expected, from Homer's occasionally farcical handling of the gods,
Aphrodite, goddess of love, had love problems herself. She was
beloved of Posiedon and herself loved Ares, the god of war. Perhaps one of the most humorous passages in the *Odyssey* describes
her irate husband catching her and Ares in the very throes of love
with a great golden net. He calls the other gods to witness the
treachery but they have a great laugh at his expense.

Apollo (or Apollon)—The god of light, healing and music in later
myth. In the *Iliad* he is a powerful and vengeful god who appears first in his Trojan identity as *Apollo Smintheus* (or "Apollo
Red Mouse"). Homer also shows him in his Greek form ("Lord
of the Silver Bow")—note that the gods take forms and guises at
will and also that the Greeks and Trojans shared generally the
same divinities even though archaeological studies have shown
a religion common to Hellas and Troad to have been most unlikely.

　　　Apollo is the son of Zeus and Leto and is the twin brother
of Artemis. He and his sister took the side of the Trojans in the
war as legend had it that he had even helped to build the walls
of the city. It was Apollo who guided Paris' arrow to Achilles' heel
later in the war. It was Apollo, too, who fell in love with Priam's
daughter Kassandra (see *Agamemnon*, above) and gave her the
gift of prophecy which became a curse when she refused him her
favors in return.

Apple of Discord—the golden apple inscribed "for the fairest," thrown
by Eris at the wedding of Thetis and Peleus; Aphrodite, Hera, and
Pallas Athena each claimed the apple. Paris was chosen the judge
of the most deserving and awarded it to Aphrodite (see COMPLETE
BACKGROUND, "Causes of The Trojan War—Mythical").

Arcadia—a beautiful, mountainous region, haunt of the god Pan, in
the Peloponnesus, west of Mycenae (see MAP, p. 5).

Ares—the god of war (later the Roman *Mars*), son of Zeus and Hera;
Zeus calls him "the most hateful of the gods." He is the lover of

Aphrodite and at her request takes the side of Troy; in the battle of the gods (Book XXI) Athena easily bests him and he goes whining to father Zeus.

Aretus—another of Priam's sons.

Argives—the men of Argos (see MAP, p. 5); the term, however, is used as a general name, like *Acheans,* to refer to the Greeks.

Artemis—goddess of the hunt, of childbirth, and of the moon; she is the twin sister of Apollo. It was Artemis whom *Agamemnon* (see above) had insulted so that she prevented him from sailing to Troy. She takes little part in the war but nevertheless sides with the Trojans.

Asklepios—son of Apollo and god of medicine and healing, father of *Makhon,* below.

Astyanax—also named Skamandros, the infant son of Hektor and Andromakhe. The realism and pathos with which he is drawn in Book VI have rarely been equaled in Western literature. At the end of the war Odysseus recommended that the child be killed— in consequence of a corraborating prophecy of Kalkhas, Astyanax was taken from his mother and thrown from the top of a Trojan tower.

Athena—See *Pallas Athena,* below.

Attica—region in central Greece whose chief city was Athens.

Automedon—Achilles' charioteer.

Balios—one of Achilles' immortal horses (see also *Xanthos,* below).

Boetia—an agriculturally rich area of central Greece whose chief city was Thebes (see MAP, p. 5).

Briseis—Woman captured by Achilles in the sack of Lyrnessos where Achilles had killed her husband and brother. Patroklos took pity on her and arranged for her to become Achilles' bedmate. Agamemnon claimed her as part of his battle spoil when Apollo's plague caused him to return the girl Khryseis to her father. Briseis is returned to Achilles (Book XIX) after the death of Patroklos.

Briseus—father of Briseis.

Danaans—another name for the Greeks in general.

Dardania—a city at the foot of Mount Ida; Homer sometimes uses Dardanians to refer to the Trojans in general.

Delphi—Greek town, place of the oracle of Apollo (see MAP, p. 5).

Demeter—goddess of grains and the mother of Persephone; she is sister of Zeus and Poseidon. Often called by the epithet "Earth-mother," she takes no part in war or violence.

Diomede—female slave of Achilles, taken from the isle of Lesbos.

Diomedes—one of the greatest Greek warriors, friend of Odysseus whom he accompanied into Troy as a spy in Book X; it is Diomedes whom Pallas Athene encourages to attack and wound Ares.

Dione—the mother of Aphrodite in some versions of the myth of her birth (see *Aphrodite,* above); she is a very old goddess and some scholars feel her to have at one time been synonymous with *Hera,* below.

Dionysos—god of wine and revelry, son of Zeus; in later Greek thought he came to symbolize the life-death cycle of the seasons, which idea transferred to the conferation of immortality upon his followers. In fifth-century Greece he seems to have been god of the theater and is often known by the epithet *dithyrambos.*

Dolon—the Trojan spy (son of Eumedes) who attempts to enter the Greek camp (Book X) on the night when Odysseus and Diomedes are on a similar mission in the Greek camp; he betrays Trojan military information to the Greeks, who thereupon kill him.

Dymas—a Phrygian king, father of Hekuba—thus the grandfather of Hektor.

Eetion—(a) a king of Thebes and father of Andromakhe—thus Hektor's father-in-law; the mythological account has it that Achilles slew him and many of his sons in an attack years before the seige of Troy; (b) father of Imbros and friend of Priam who had been instrumental in the ransom of his son, Lycaon.

Ennomus—(a) an augur or seer, chief of the Mysians, he is slain by Achilles; (b) a Trojan slain by Odysseus.

Eos—goddess of the dawn and wife of Tithonos—she has rosy fingers and toes—"the rosy fingered dawn" being one of the best-known formulas in Homer.

Erubus—(a) that part of the lower world through which the soul must pass to enter the Kingdom of Hades, (b) a general term for "darkness."

Eris—goddess of Discord (see *Apple of Discord,* above).

Erinys—an avenging supernatural being, sometimes shown in the shape of a great bird with a woman's head. Referred to by the epithet "she who walks in mist." Not even the gods were exempt from the avenging fury of the Erinys.

Erymas—a Trojan slain by Patroklos in Book XVI.

Euboea—large island off the eastern coast of Attica (see MAP, p.5), the largest Greek island in the Aegean.

Euphorbos—one of the three killers of Patroklos, at the end of Book XVI. He is described by Melelaos in Book XVII; his death is narrated in elaborate detail.

Eurymedon—(a) Agamemnon's squire, (b) a servant of Nestor.

Ganymede—son of Tros (the founder of Troy); he was said to be so beautiful a boy that he was taken to Olympos to be Zeus' cup-bearer.

Granicus—a river with its sources on Mt. Ida.

Hades (*or Aides or Aidoneus*)—brother of Zeus and ruler of the world of the dead (he becomes "Dis" in the Roman tradition; in some Greek myth he is called "Pluto").

Hebe—wife of Heracles, daughter of Zeus, the goddess of youth and spring.

Hektor—see CHARACTER ANALYSIS, "Trojans."

Hekuba (*or Hekabe*)—mother of Hektor and Paris; wife of Priam. With the fall of Troy, legends contend that she was awarded as a prize to Odysseus but that she was transformed into a bitch and would thus never have been carried captive to Greece as was her daughter Kassandra (see *Agamemnon,* above).

Helen—see CHARACTER ANALYSIS, "Greeks."

Helenus—son of Priam.

Helios Hyperion—the sun.

Hellas—a name for all of Greece.

Hellespont—the channel which links the Aegean with the Black Sea; Troy is at the western end (see MAP, p. 5).

Hephaistos—god of fire and metallurgy, son of Zeus. He has a prominent role in the *Iliad* as a participant on the Greek side and as the maker of Achilles' armor. He was lame and ugly and married to Kharis or Aphrodite, the goddess of love. As god of fire it is significant to the *Iliad's* fire-water conflict (see CRITICAL ANALYSIS) that Hephaistos could rarely be brought to use his divine skills for other than peaceful ends (he later becomes the Roman "Vulcan").

Hera—sister and wife of Zeus, queen of the gods and goddess of marriage and families (she is "Juno" in the Roman tradition). In the Trojan War she is pro-Greek and her subsequent machinations lead to many of the Iliad's comic situations. Homer has given her a round and fully developed character: Skillful in persuading

Zeus, something of a shrew, always determined to get her way. She is known frequently by the epithets "white-armed" and "ox-eyed." According to Homer, the Greek cities Argos, Mycenae, and Sparta were her beloved favorites; she is also on the side of the Greeks as Paris hadn't awarded her the golden *Apple of Discord* (above).

Herakles—son of Zeus (his name means the "glory of Hera"), the legendary performer of the twelve labors. He built the famous Pillars of Herakles and was later known to the Romans as *Hercules.*

Hermes—god of thieves and of commerce; considered to be the guide of souls into the realm of Hades (he was also the bringer of dreams), Homer has him guide Priam across the dark plain to Achilles where he begs for the body of his son. In later myth (and in the *Odyssey*) he is the messenger of Zeus, an office taken in the *Iliad* by Iris.

Hyperion—see *Helios,* above.

Ida— mountain range in the Troad, see MAP, p. 5. Mt. Ida is used by Homer as Zeus' "home away from home," the grandstand from which he oversaw the war.

Idomeneus—leader of the Cretan forces. He is getting old (his hair is gray); as "Lord of Crete" he is one of the most important of the commanders, Crete and Mycenae (Agamemnon's city) being the principal powers of the Panhellenic world at this time.

Ilioneus—the Trojan warrior whom Peneleus slays brutally.

Ilium—another name for Troy.

Ilus—son of Tros and the grandfather of Priam; the builder of Troy.

Iris—the rainbow and the messenger of Zeus in the *Iliad.*

Ithaka—the Kingdom of Odysseus.

Kalkhas—Greek priest and prophet or seer, who, in Book I, advises Agamemnon that Apollo has sent the plague because of Agamemnon's having taken the daughter of Khryses (a priest of Apollo) captive; (see *Khryseis*).

Kassandra—daughter of Priam and Hekuba, brother of Paris; a prophetess taken captive to Greece by Agamemnon (see *Apollo,* above). She has a minor role in the *Iliad* (she is the first to see Priam returning with the body of Hektor) but she has an important place in the myths of Troy later (see Vergil's *Aeneid* and Aeschylus' *Agamemnon*). Her name has come to mean that of a prophet whom no one will believe.

Kastor—brother of Helen.

Kebriones—Hektor's charioteer, slain by Patroklos in Book XVI.

Khryseis—Agamemnon's female prize of war; he is forced to return her to her father on the advice of Kalchas in Book I that (as she is the daughter of a priest of Apollo) her captivity is the cause of the plague among the Greeks.

Khryses—father of Khryseis and priest of Apollo at *Khryse,* a harbor settlement in the Troad.

Klaitemnestra—wife of *Agamemnon* (see above) who stabs him to death on his return from Troy.

Kronos—son of Uranos, father of the Olympian gods. He was dethroned by Zeus, Hades, and Poseidon, who then divided his universe among themselves—Zeus taking the sky, Hades the underworld, and Poseidon the Sea.

Laërtes—father of Odysseus.

Lampos—Hektor's horse.

Laomedon—father of Priam.

Leitus—leader of the Boeotians; wounded by Hektor in the fight for possession of Patroklos' body in Book XVII.

Lemnos—island due west of Troy, sacred to Hephaistos. The Greek force stopped here according to tradition on its way to Troy (see MAP, p. 5).

Lesbos—island south-west of Troad; a part of Priam's kingdom, Achilles' forces had earlier assaulted and captured the island.

Leto—by Zeus, the mother of Apollo and Artemis. In Greek myth, Leto was insulted by Niobe who boasted of *her* fine children; Leto called upon Apollo and his sister to avenge her and they promptly killed Niobe's seven sons and seven daughters.

Lykaon—a son of Priam, slain by Achilles.

Makhon—physician to the Greeks and son of the god of healing, Asklepios. Nestor saves him on the battlefield when he is wounded in Book XI.

Menelaos—King of Sparta, husband of Helen, and brother of Agamemnon (see CHARACTER ANALYSIS).

Minos—legendary King of Crete at Knossos; in Homer, Minos is a judge of the dead.

Mycenae—Agamemnon's city (see MAP, p. 5).

Myrmidons—warriors under the leadership of Achilles.

Neoptolemus—son of Achilles; following Achilles' death he went to battle in his father's armor and, after the entry into the city by the device of Odysseus' wooden horse, Neoptolemus is said to have been the one to behead Priam.

Nereus—father of Thetis and thus grandfather of Achilles; he is a minor sea deity.

Nestor—Agamemnon's advisor; see CHARACTER ANALYSIS, "Greeks."

Odios—(a) a chief of the Halizones, slain by Agamemnon in Book V, (b) a Greek herald.

Odysseus—son of Laërtes and often called by the epithet "crafty," he is the wiliest of the Greek leaders; he was later honored by the award of Achilles' armor. Following the sack of Troy, Odysseus sets sail for his home Ithaka and his wife Penelope but is prevented by Poseidon (who had been on the Greek side in the Trojan War) from returning for ten years because of Odysseus' blinding of the sea god's son, Polyphemos, the Cyclops. The ten years' adventures constitute much of the *Odyssey*.

Olympos—mountain in Thessaly (see MAP, p.5) held by the Greeks to be the home of their gods.

Orestes—(a) a Greek slain by Hektor, (b) in Aeschylus' play, the son of *Agamemnon* and Klaitemnestra, who kills his mother (and her lover) for her murder of his father.

Pallas Athene (or Athena)—goddess of wisdom and, with Hera, the chief divine aid of the Greeks. Known by the epithet "bright-eyed," she is enemy to Paris and the Trojans because of the judgement of Paris (see COMPLETE BACKGROUND, p. xx). Odysseus, Achilles, and Diomedes are her favorites.

Pandaros—Lycian archer slain by Diomedes in Book V; he breaks the truce between the armies in Book IV by shooting Menelaos.

Paris Alexander—son of Priam, prince of Troy (see CHARACTER ANALYSIS).

Patroklos—friend of Achilles, slain by Hektor (see CHARACTER ANALYSIS).

Pedasos—Achilles' mortal horse killed by Sarpedon in Book XVI.

Peisander—(a) a leader of Achilles' Myrmidons, (b) a Trojan slain by Agamemnon, (c) Trojan slain by Menelaos.

Peleus—father of Achilles, husband of the sea nymph Thetis.

Pelops—the grandfather of Agamemnon and Menelaus (and Aegisthus—lover of Agamemnon's wife Klaitemnestra); Pelops is the son of Tantalos.

Persephone—queen of the dead, wife of Hades, daughter of Demeter. In Greek mythology she is carried off by Hades causing the great sorrow of Demeter (goddess of fertility) and a resultant winter on earth. Persephone regularly returns from the underworld to visit his mother, thus the cycle of the seasons.

Philoktetes—warrior abandoned on *Lemnos* (above) on the Greek expedition's way to Troy. He had been bitten by a snake and the foul wound would not heal so that he remained on Lemnos with the famous bow and arrows of Herakles. Philoktetes had later to be brought to Troy to ensure its capture according to prophecy. Sophocles' drama, the *Philoktetes*, deals with the episode of Odysseus and Neoptolemos bringing him to Troy.

Phoinix—Achilles' childhood teacher, nurse, and companion. Now that he is old, he commands a battalion of Myrmidons. Phoinix is one of the ambassadors sent by Agamemnon to persuade Achilles to relent in his anger and rejoin the battle.

Phorbas—King of Lesbos.

Phrygia—region south of the Hellespont, due east of Troad.

Phthia—Achille's domain in Thessaly.

Polydoros—the youngest son of Priam, he is killed by Achilles in Book XX.

Poseidon—god of the sea, brother of Zeus and Hades, he is known by the epithets "Holder of the earth" and "Earth-shaker." Later to become the Roman *Neptune*, he lives in an underwater palace near Euboea and, in the Trojan War, assists the Greeks whenever Zeus turns his back.

Poulydamas—son of Panthous, he is a speaker at several Trojan councils. He is cautious and fears that Hektor's extension of the war onto the plain and behind the Greek wall is unwise.

Priam—King of Troy (see CHARACTER ANALYSIS).

Pylaemenes—a Paphlagonian slain by Menelaus in Book V; this seems to slip Homer's mind and Pylaemenes reappears quite alive in Book XIII. Other characters with whom this happens are *Khromios* and *Skhedios*.

Pylos—Nestor's city (see MAP, p. 5).

Salamis—island near Athens, the home of Ajax. Salamis is later the scene of the decisive sea battle between the Athenian navy and that of the Persian Xerxes in 480 B.C.

Sarpedon—a leader of the Lycians, a warrior of great skill and courage (and a son of Zeus), slain by Patroklos in Book XVI and there is a great fight to reclaim his body.

Skaian Gate—the gates of Troy facing the plain and the Greek encampment.

Skamander—a river flowing from Ida, by Troy, into the Aegean.

Skamandros—(a) see *Astyanax*, above, (b) a Trojan slain by Menelaos in Book V.

Simois—a stream flowing into the Skamander.

Sparta—capital city of Lacedaemon, the kingdom of Menelaos.

Styx—river in the underworld, so sacred that the gods often make their oaths by it.

Talthybios—Agamemnon's herald.

Telemachus—son of Odysseus and Penelope.

Teucer—best of the Greek archers, he is the brother of Ajax and son of Telamon.

Theano—a priestess of Athena in Troy.

Thebes—(a) city in Boetia, ancient kingdom of Oedipus, (b) a city in the Troad (also a city far up the Nile in Egypt).

Thessaly—region north of Boetia   (see MAP, p. 5),   location of Mount Olympos.

Thetis—the wife of Peleus and mother of Achilles. In Greek myth it was prophesied that she would bear a son more famous than his father; Zeus, who had been seeking her favor, promptly denied himself the pleasure of her.

Themis—goddess of law and custom.

Thersites—a common Greek soldier whose criticism of Agamemnon is the *Iliad's* "voice of the people"; Odysseus beats him for his outspokenness.

Thrace—see MAP, p. 5;   region north-east of Macedonia and held to be the home of Ares. In the Trojan War the Thracians are allies of King Priam.

Thrasymedes—son of Nestor.

Troad—that region of Asia Minor of which Troy is the chief city.

Trolilus—son of Priam (a European, medieval singer later makes him the lover of Cressida, a daughter of Kalkhas).

Tros—(a) great grandfather of Priam; the father of Ilus who was the builder of Troy; (b) a Trojan slain by Achilles in Book XX.

Xanthos—(a) a Trojan slain by Diomedes in Book V, (b) one of
Achilles' immortal horses, (c) a river in Lycia, (d) name often
used for the Skamander.

Zeus—father of the gods and of men. His power among the gods is
physical (as he himself had dethroned his father Kronos). His
spiritual powers, however, are decidedly human, and Homer gives
him dimensions of a good man who has an extraordinarily tempestu-
ous family (and a tragic and complex world of men) to look after
and lead toward righteousness and balance as best he can—in his
typical role as mediator he had referred Athena, Hera, and Aphrodite to Paris for the decision as to who would be awarded the
golden apple of Discord. During the last year of the Trojan War
he is determined to remain impartial and warns that all the gods
must do the same—as usual they interfere whenever he is looking in
the other direction. A sky-god, he is known by many epithets: "high-
throned," "aegis-bearing," "Lord of lightning," "dark-clouded."
Zeus later became the Roman *Jupiter*.

NOTES

NOTES

NOTES

NOTES

NOTES